GOVERNMENT PROCEDURES AND OPERATIONS

LOBBYING REGULATION

HISTORY, LAWS, REFORM OPTIONS, AND COMPLIANCE

Government Procedures and Operations

Additional books in this series can be found on Nova's website under the Series tab.

Additional e-books in this series can be found on Nova's website under the eBooks tab.

GOVERNMENT PROCEDURES AND OPERATIONS

LOBBYING REGULATION

HISTORY, LAWS, REFORM OPTIONS, AND COMPLIANCE

WILLARD N. SIMMONS
EDITOR

New York

Library of Congress Cataloging-in-Publication Data

ISBN: 978-1-63484-998-2

Published by Nova Science Publishers, Inc. † New York

CONTENTS

PREFACE

This book provides a retrospective and prospective analysis of the Lobbying Disclosure Act (LDA) on its 20th anniversary. It begins with a historical summary of citizens' right to petition, the connection between the right to petition and lobbying, and the regulation of contact between citizens and government in the United States. The book then examines contemporary issues that might affect lobbying and citizens' right to petition government; and provides analysis of potential options for congressional action should Congress consider amending provisions of the LDA. Moreover, the book provides a brief history and description of the provisions of federal law restricting employment opportunities and activities of federal employees after they leave the service of the executive or legislative branches of the federal government.

In: Lobbying Regulation
Editor: Willard N. Simmons
ISBN: 978-1-63484-998-2

Chapter 1

THE LOBBYING DISCLOSURE ACT AT 20: ANALYSIS AND ISSUES FOR CONGRESS*

Jacob R. Straus

SUMMARY

On December 19, 1995, President William Jefferson Clinton signed the Lobbying Disclosure Act (LDA) into law (2 U.S.C. §1601, *et seq.*). In his comments when signing the law, President Clinton identified a central question that continues to be an issue for lobbying laws: how can individual citizens' rights be balanced against the desire to regulate and potentially control the access of special interests to government? As lobbying laws have been developed in the United States, the balance between the right of "ordinary Americans" to petition the government and the access that professional lobbyists can have to Members of Congress and executive branch decisionmakers has been at the forefront.

The four major federal lobbying laws—the Foreign Agents Registration Act (FARA) of 1938, the Regulation of Lobbying Act (RLA) of 1946, the Lobbying Disclosure Act (LDA) of 1995, and the Honest Leadership and Open Government Act (HLOGA) of 2007—were enacted in response to changes in practice or perception surrounding lobbying. In most cases, the enactment, repeal, or amendment of lobbying laws was a response to multiple contextual changes that provided a policy window in which change was possible.

---

* This is an edited, reformatted and augmented version of a Congressional Research Service publication, No. R44292, dated December 1, 2015.

This report provides a retrospective and prospective analysis of the LDA on its 20th anniversary, using research conducted and data collected by the Bush School of Government and Public Service at Texas A&M capstone class over the 2014-2015 academic year. As the LDA turns 20, several issues, each already addressed to some extent in other statutes, have the potential to cause additional shifts in lobbying practices and perception. These include

- *Shadow lobbying*—when an individual who is paid to engage public officials on behalf of clients does not register as a lobbyist. Shadow lobbying may raise questions about what practices and activities should trigger lobbyist registration requirements.
- *Grassroots lobbying*—attempts to persuade government decisionmakers and influence policy outcomes by shifting public opinion and motivating citizens to take action, often by contacting Representatives and Senators. Grassroots lobbying is generally unregulated, although legislation has been introduced in the past that would require grassroots lobbying activities be registered and disclosed.
- *Revolving door*—when federal employees leave the government for employment in the private sector or the government hires former private sector employees for government jobs. There are a number of post-employment restrictions that impose limits on federal employees moving to the private sector, or former lobbyists moving to the public sector. Analysis of whether current restrictions strike a suitable balance, are too restrictive, or too permissive, may be instructive.

As these issues evolve, Congress has many options available to potentially amend existing lobbying laws. These include options to

- change the definition of lobbying;
- change disclosure thresholds for registered lobbyists; and
- adjust resources available for implementation and enforcement.

Additionally, Congress could choose not to amend existing lobbying laws and maintain current standards.

INTRODUCTION

On December 19, 1995, the Lobbying Disclosure Act (LDA) became law.[1] Upon signing the LDA into law, President William Jefferson Clinton endorsed lobbying as a basic American right, while also providing context as to why such a law is necessary for a transparent and open government.

> Lobbying has its rightful place in our system. I believe every Member here and every Member who voted for this bill understands that and understands what a valuable role lobbying can play in the American system. At one time or another, just about every American citizen has wanted to be a lobbyist before the Congress on one issue or another.
>
> But ordinary Americans also understand that organized interests too often can hold too much sway in the halls of power. They know that in Washington an influence industry too often operates in secret and gets special privileges not available to most Americans. Lobbyists in the back room secretly rewriting laws and looking for loopholes do not have a place in our democracy. All the people should know what is done by people who affect public decisions.[2]

Commenting on the disparity between the right of "ordinary Americans" to petition the government and the access that professional lobbyists can have to Members of Congress and executive branch decisionmakers, President Clinton identified a central question: how can individual citizens' rights be balanced against the desire to regulate and potentially control the access of special interests to government?

Questions of access have often been asked, perhaps most prominently in American history by James Madison in the *Federalist Papers*. Madison called groups of individuals "who are united and actuated by some common impulse ... or interest," factions and recognized they had the right to form and advocate for their interests.[3] To address the potentially negative role of factions, or organized interests, Madison believed that two solutions existed: ban the formation of groups or encourage the existence of multiple groups. He advocated for the latter—allowing groups to proliferate so that no one group can dominate.

Translated to lobbying, the Madisonian ideal to provide all citizens the ability to contact government and express opinions has resulted in lobbying laws that focus on registration and disclosure—activities that do not impinge on the constitutional rights of citizens.[4] Requiring the registration of lobbyists and the disclosure of lobbying activities, rather than banning lobbying, can ensure that all citizens continue to have access to government and a protected right to petition.

This report provides a retrospective and prospective analysis of the LDA on its 20th anniversary. It begins with a historical summary of citizens' right to petition, the connection between the right to petition and lobbying, and the regulation of contact between citizens and government in the United States. The report then examines contemporary issues that might affect lobbying and citizens' right to petition government. Finally, the report concludes with an analysis of potential options for congressional action should Congress consider amending provisions of the LDA.

REGULATING LOBBYING

The tension between the right to petition the government and the regulation of access to policymakers has played an essential role in how lobbying has been managed. In an effort to balance these needs, Congress has historically created boundaries to the right to petition that have required the registration of individuals who represent interest groups before Congress and the executive branch. This registration requires the public disclosure of certain lobbying activities. Additionally, Congress has focused on ensuring that no single group has an undue advantage over other groups by creating rules that prohibit the acceptance of gifts by government officials from certain individuals (e.g., lobbyists) and placing limits and restrictions on the post-congressional activities of Members of Congress and senior staff.[5]

Historic Rights to Petition

The right of citizens to petition government has long been considered a protected and fundamental aspect of the citizen-government dynamic. Long before the establishment of the United States, English common law afforded citizens the right to petition the Crown for grievances.[6] Following its English heritage, the United States has employed a similar structure. The right to petition government came with the colonists to the New World and became ingrained in colonial life.[7]

The right to petition government was so deeply rooted in American life, that while it was not explicitly addressed in the Constitution,[8] it was immediately included in the Bill of Rights.[9] In the early years of the Constitution, the right to petition government featured prominently in several debates. For example, in January 1790, Benjamin Franklin sent a petition to

Congress "calling for the federal government to put an immediate end to the African slave trade."[10] His petition prompted an intense debate over slavery in the House.[11] The right to petition was also noted by French scholar Alexis de Tocqueville during his travel around the United States in the 1830s, where he observed that political associations could provide individuals a voice in society and government that they would otherwise not enjoy.[12]

Modern Definition of Lobbying and Lobbyists

In a modern context, the right to petition government is often viewed through the lens of an organized group's desire to present positions to governmental decisionmakers. Most often, this involves hiring lobbyists to represent and advocate for the groups' policy preferences. The Lobbying Disclosure Act of 1995 defines lobbying as

> oral or written communication (including an electronic communication) to a covered executive branch official or a covered legislative branch official that is made on behalf of a client with the regard to
>
> I. the formulation, modification, or adoption of Federal legislation (including legislative proposals);
> II. the formulation, modification, or adoption of a Federal rule, regulation, Executive order, or any other program, policy, or position of the United States Government;
> III. the administration or execution of a Federal program or policy (including the negotiation, award, or administration of a Federal contract, grant, loan, permit, or license); or
> IV. the nomination or confirmation of a person for a position subject to confirmation by the Senate.[13]

Lobbyists—individuals who engage in lobbying—are further defined as individuals who are "employed or retained by a client for financial or other compensation for services that include more than one lobbying contact, other than an individual whose lobbying activities constitute less than 20% of the time engaged in the services provided by such individual to that client over a 3-month period."[14]

An individual must meet all three of these criteria to be a lobbyist. If an individual does not make more than one lobbying contact in a quarterly period, spend at least 20% of his or her time lobbying, and receive compensation, he or she is not considered a lobbyist. Further, if an individual is not contacting specific executive or legislative branch officials,[15] then he or she is not considered a lobbyist under the law.

Lobbying Goals

Lobbyists perform a variety of tasks for their clients. Whether they represent corporations, individual citizens, or interest groups, lobbyists attempt to influence the policy process and secure desired outcomes for clients. In general, groups may decide to lobby for several reasons, including to provide information, to persuade, and to signal positions or policy preferences.

Choosing whether to contact the legislative or executive branch depends on the type of action sought.[16] The legislative branch formulates the law, and lobbyists can use contact with covered legislative branch officials—Members of Congress, elected officers of the House and Senate, and congressional staff—to push for new laws or amendments to existing laws.[17] The executive branch implements the law, and lobbyists can use contact with covered executive branch officials—the President, Vice-President, employees of the Executive Office of the President, Cabinet secretaries, and senior executive branch and military officials—to advocate for or against regulations and implementation practices for existing laws.[18]

Since the Constitution was ratified in 1789, individuals have looked to provide information to government decisionmakers. Political scientist Anthony Nownes has found that lobbyists generally provide three types of information to decisionmakers:

> (1) *political information* about the status and prospect of a proposed or potential government decision; (2) *career-related information* about the implications of a particular course of action for a government official's prospects of keeping and/or advancing in his or her job; and (3) *policy-analytic information* about the potential economic, social, or environmental consequences of a particular course of action.[19]

Information is arguably a lobbyist's key commodity.[20] Senator Robert Byrd, during a lecture on lobbying delivered to the Senate, stated that "despite the criticism of lobbyists, nineteenth century Senators came to appreciate the help they could offer."[21] Even then, and absent the type of professional staff that Members of Congress currently enjoy, Senators looked to lobbyists for assistance in parsing information and policy options.[22]

Lobbyists may also work to persuade.[23] Senator Byrd further recounted that as early as 1795, "a Philadelphia newspaper described the way lobbyists waited outside Congress Hall to 'give a hint to a Member ... or advise as may best suit.'"[24] Lobbyists, because of their positions outside the government, have the ability to view the policy sphere holistically and provide factual information on policy preferences, as well as consider non-policy factors, including reelection and the use of "information about constituency views ... to persuade legislators that electoral self-interest lies in taking group-friendly positions."[25]

Lastly, lobbyists can signal what affiliated group members might think about a particular issue. Most often, signaling occurs through advertisements or grassroots campaigns—where a group asks its members to contact Members of Congress to express an opinion.[26] Signaling is an important lobbying tool. Some academic studies have observed a positive, and sometimes strong, correlation between money spent on advertising, grassroots campaigns, and campaign contributions with policy influence.[27] Other studies have found that signaling is of "modest value" as a lobbying tool.[28]

Framing the Regulation of Lobbying

At various points in American history, there have been shifts in the way lobbying has been practiced and perceived. In turn, these changes have led to new attempts to regulate lobbying and interest group influence. Changes in practice include how lobbyists conduct business and the types and scope of contacts with the legislative and executive branch. Changes in perception include shifts in societal norms about what lobbyists should or should not be doing.

Regulation of lobbying has frequently been used as a political tool, especially in the early 20th century. Senator Robert Byrd stated,

> Progressive presidents like Theodore Roosevelt and Woodrow Wilson took advantage of ... popular images of lobbyists and business corruption as leverage for their reform legislation. In seeking public support for lower tariff rates, President Wilson trained his fire on the lobby with this sharply worded attack: "Washington has seldom seen so numerous, so industrious or so insidious a body. The newspapers are

being filled with paid advertisements calculated to mislead the judgment of public men not only, but also the public opinion of the country itself."[29]

Senator Byrd's summary of the historic reasons for lobbying reform in many ways mirrors why change might take place in contemporary politics. Lobbying reform has historically focused on the registration of lobbyists and the disclosure of lobbying activities. This focus, rather than on curtailing lobbying activities, has arguably allowed Congress to avoid potential constitutional concerns over lobbying as a manifestation of citizens' First Amendment right to petition the government.[30]

Historically, the focus has not been on radical lobbying reform. Instead, lobbying laws have focused on the registration of lobbyists and the disclosure of their activities. The changes that have been enacted have arisen are often the result of what political scientist John Kingdon described as the opening of a policy window.[31] Put more plainly, change can occur when a crisis develops that allows governmental decisionmakers to seize the opportunity to make change. For example, the Foreign Agent Registration Act (FARA) was enacted in response to concerns about German interests being represented prior to World War II,[32] and the Honest Leadership and Open Government Act (HLOGA) was enacted partly in response to the Jack Abramoff scandal.[33]

LOBBYING LAWS

Even before the first lobbying law was enacted, Congress made numerous attempts—some adopted, some not—to bring transparency to lobbying. For example, in 1876, after a bill reported by the House Judiciary Committee was only "argued at the request of an important corporation,"[34] the House required lobbyists to register with the Clerk of the House. This requirement, however, was only effective for the 44th Congress (1875-1877).[35]

Since the 1930s, four key laws have been enacted to regulate, but not ban, lobbyist contact with the federal government. Through an examination of these laws, it becomes clear that each was precipitated by changes in the practice of lobbying or political perception of lobbyists and their activities. The four primary lobbying laws are

- the Foreign Agent Registration Act (FARA) of 1938;[36]
- the Regulation of Lobbying Act (RLA) of 1946;[37]

- the Lobbying Disclosure Act (LDA) of 1995;[38] and
- the Honest Leadership and Open Government Act (HLOGA) of 2007.[39]

Foreign Agent Registration Act of 1938

In 1938, the Foreign Agents Registration Act (FARA) was enacted,[40] in an effort to "control subversive activities and propaganda dissemination by Nazi and Communist agents in the United States."[41] Prior to the passage of FARA, the House Judiciary Committee issued a report to accompany the legislation (H.R. 1591) that addressed the severity of the issue.

> This bill was introduced as a result of recommendations of the special committee that was appointed by the Seventy-third Congress to investigate un-American activities in the United States. A very careful study was made of the organizations in this country[,] which organizations aimed arbitrarily to group certain American citizens and persons in the U.S., and teachings in these positions to influence the internal and external political policies of our country.
>
> Incontrovertible evidence has been submitted to prove that there are many persons in the United States representing foreign governments or foreign political groups, who are supplied by such foreign agencies with funds and other materials to foster un-American activities, and to influence the external and internal policies of this country, thereby violating both the letter and the spirit of international law, as well as the democratic basis of our own American institution of government.[42]

FARA requires the registration of "any person who acts as an agent, representative, employee, or servant, or any person who acts in any other capacity at the order, request, or under the direction or control, of a foreign principal.... "[43] Additionally, FARA

- specifies how such agents are to register and report their activities;[44]
- exempts certain types of foreign agents from registration;[45]
- has specific filing and labeling requirements for political propaganda disseminated by registered agents;[46]
- requires all registered agents to preserve records and to make these records available for inspection by the Department of Justice;[47]

- provides for public examination of registration statements, reports, and political propaganda filed with the Department of Justice;[48] and
- imposes penalties for noncompliance.[49]

The passage of FARA was a direct response to the perception of foreign influence in the United States. In the climate surrounding the rise of the Nazi Party in Germany and general unrest in both Europe and Asia, Congress felt it necessary to pass a law that dealt with the perception that foreign agents had undue influence over American foreign policy and growing concern over how conflict in Europe and Asia might influence both American politics and general civil society.[50] FARA may also be viewed as a predecessor to modern lobbying laws.

The Regulation of Lobbying Act of 1946

In 1946, as part of the Legislative Reorganization Act (Title III, the "Regulation of Lobbying Act" (RLA)), Congress required that "any person who shall engage himself for pay or for any consideration for the purpose of attempting to influence the passage or defeat of any legislation by the Congress of the United States"[51] register with the Clerk of the House and the Secretary of the Senate and disclose activities. The RLA was effective in creating the first general registration and disclosure regime.

As the *Yale Law Journal* stated in summarizing the legislative process used to regulate lobbying, prior to 1946, with the RLA Congress was responding to how lobbyists were viewed within the larger society when crafting the RLA:

> Whereas the old-style lobby, confined almost entirely to representatives of business interests, operated secretly and depended for its success upon personal solicitation of legislators, often accompanied by corruption, such methods are largely obsolete today. Modern lobbyists, or legislative agents, act on behalf of almost every conceivable business, economic, and social group, generally operate openly and frankly, and rely upon public opinion, real or simulated through judicious use of publicity and propaganda, to compel legislative action.[52]

In its report on the underlying legislation, the Senate Special Committee on the Organization of Congress provided a rationale for requiring lobbyists to register their activities.[53]

> Congress is the center of political gravity under our form of government because it reflects and expresses the popular will in making of national policy. Too often, however, the true attitude of public opinion is distorted and obscured by the pressures of special-interest groups. Beset by swarms of lobbyists seeking to protect this or that small segment of the economy or to advance this or that narrow interest, legislators find it difficult to discover the real majority will and to legislate in the public interest.[54]

The committee believed that the registration of lobbyists and disclosure of receipts and expenditures would allow lobbying to continue and would avoid "impairing in any way the right of petition or freedom of expression" for individuals.[55] Overall, "the act was not intended to regulate lobbying or restrict the legislative activities of particular individuals or organizations, rather, through recordkeeping, registration, and reporting requirements, the act seeks public disclosure of the identity and financial interests of persons engaged in lobbying."[56] Additionally, the RLA attempted to reduce the potential for undue influence by lobbyists on the legislative process.[57]

After enactment, some number of lobbyists who were attempting to influence legislation in Congress registered with the Clerk and the Secretary. Studies of the RLA have shown, however, that the number of registered lobbyists likely did not match the number of individuals and organizations that were actively working to influence legislation as their primary mission ("principal purpose").[58]

Part of the reason for the RLA's weakness was the Supreme Court's decision in *United States v. Harriss* (1954).[59] The Court "upheld ... lobbying registration requirements.... The Court defined the legislation narrowly, however, finding that it did not apply to groups or individuals who spent their own money to lobby Congress directly. It also exempted groups whose principal purpose was something other than lobbying."[60] Subsequently, some observed that the original intent of the law—to require the registration and disclosure "to identify financial interest of person[s] engaged in lobbying"[61]—was ineffective.

Over the next several decades, various legislative attempts were made to amend or replace the RLA. For example, in 1976, the Senate drafted and passed "more specific definitions of lobbyists and lobbying practices, but intensive efforts by lobbyists—principally arguing that the new requirements would violate the free speech rights of lobbyists—kept the measure from passing the House."[62]

The Lobbying Disclosure Act of 1995

The RLA, in the post-*Harriss* era, was considered by many to be "unsatisfactory," with limited effectiveness.[63] The RLA, coupled with competing registration and disclosure standards in at least six different statutes, prompted Congress to create a new, more comprehensive registration and disclosure scheme.[64] The result was the Lobbying Disclosure Act (LDA) of 1995. Described on the Senate floor as "the right balance," the LDA "tightens up the registration and disclosure requirements for the Washington-based lobbyists, without infringing upon the rights of ordinary citizens at the grassroots to petition their Government."[65] The LDA was passed to counter "the perception that Congress in particular is beholden to special interests and that ordinary people cannot rise above the din of lobbyists having special access to and currying favor from Members of Congress or top officials in the executive branch."[66]

In addition to attempting to alter the public perception of lobbying, the LDA also served to repeal the RLA and streamline the registration and disclosure process. In reporting the LDA, the House Judiciary Committee summarized the need for new lobbying provisions:

> The Act is designed to strengthen public confidence in government by replacing the existing patchwork of lobbying disclosure laws with a single, uniform statute which covers the activities of all professional lobbyists. The Act streamlines disclosure requirements to ensure that meaningful information is provided and requires all professional lobbyists to register and file regular, semiannual reports identifying their clients, the issues on which they lobby, and the amount of their compensation. It also creates a more effective and equitable system for administering and enforcing the disclosure requirements.[67]

After passing the Senate in July 1995 and the House in November,[68] on December 19, 1995, the LDA was signed into law by President Clinton.[69] In addition to repealing the RLA, the LDA provided specific thresholds and definitions of lobbyists, lobbying activities, and lobbying contacts; and required that lobbyists register with the Clerk of the House and Secretary of the Senate.[70] The LDA broadly defined a lobbyist as an individual who is

1. employed or retained by a client for financial or other compensation[;]
2. for services that include more than one *lobbying contact*,[71] and[;]
3. his or her *lobbying activities* for that client must amount to 20 percent or more of the time that the individual expends on services to that client over a six-month period.[72]

Additionally, for the first time, executive branch officers and certain other executive branch employees were considered to be "covered officials" for the purpose of lobbying registration and disclosure.[73] Recognizing that lobbyists were also contacting executive branch officials to influence the implementation of laws and the writing of regulations was an acknowledgement that "the members of the executive branch are subject to the same lobbying, and the same influences because decisions of enormous consequence are made in the executive branch."[74]

The inclusion of executive branch employees reflected a change in how lobbyists achieve their goals, but also acknowledged that policymaking includes more than just Congress.[75] The role of the executive branch and how regulations are written can be important for lobbyists as they represent the best interests of their clients.

The Honest Leadership and Open Government Act of 2007

The most recent amendment to the LDA, the Honest Leadership and Open Government Act of 2007 (HLOGA), mandated additional and more frequent information disclosures by lobbyists.[76] Introduced in the wake of the Jack Abramoff scandal, HLOGA amended the LDA to further refine registration thresholds and definitions of lobbying activities, change the frequency of reporting, add additional disclosures, create new semi-annual reports on campaign contributions, and require disclosure by coalitions and associations.[77] Additionally, registration and disclosure statements were required to be provided in a searchable and sortable format, on the Internet, for public inspection.[78]

HLOGA was not primarily intended to increase the number of persons who are required to register and report as "lobbyists" under the LDA. Thus, the definitions of who is a covered "lobbyist," and what are "lobbying contacts" and "lobbying activities"—and therefore who must register and report under the law—were not substantively amended by the 2007 act.[79] Instead, HLOGA amended the frequency of required information disclosure and the monetary thresholds for reporting lobbying expenses or income. HLOGA created quarterly, instead of semi-annual, reporting periods and shortened the deadline for submission from 45 days to 20 days after the filing period ends.[80] The threshold for filing quarterly reports was also lowered, requiring lobbyists and lobbying firms to file reports of work when total income from lobbying exceeded $2,500 (formerly $5,000) and where total expenses used in connection with lobbying exceeded $10,000 (formerly $20,000) for any given quarterly reporting period.[81] Additionally, the LDA was amended to create a new semi-annual reporting requirement for campaign and presidential library contributions by lobbyists and lobbying firms.[82]

HLOGA was primarily a response to changes in both practice and perception. In practice, social media had also changed the way that lobbyists communicated with covered officials. Modern politics is a fast-paced environment, and lobbyists have developed myriad opportunities to directly contact Members of Congress and motivate grassroots campaigns.

Additionally, HLOGA sought to address the appearance of scandal. HLOGA, for example, banned gifts from lobbyists to Members of Congress and congressional staff. HLOGA further required greater disclosure of lobbyists' activities by the lobbyists. For government employees, including Members of Congress, financial disclosure rules were tightened and restrictions were placed on seeking employment outside of government.[83]

Common Themes in Lobbying Laws

A common theme underlies the four major lobbying laws: more information on lobbying contacts and activities increases transparency. Additionally, by requiring registration and disclosure but not restricting activities, individuals' first amendment rights to petition are maintained. **Table 1** summarizes the four lobbying laws—FARA, the RLA, the LDA, and HLOGA—and who is required to register, what they are required to disclose, how often filings are to occur, and how information is to be provided to the public.

Table 1. Registration and Disclosure Requirements under Lobbying Statutes

	Registration of Whom	Disclosure of What	How Often	How Public
Federal Agent Registration Act (FARA) P.L. 75-583, 52 Stat. 631,June 8, 1938 22 U.S.C. §§611-621	Agents of foreign governments; political parties; and partnerships, associations, corporations, organizations, or "other combination[s] of person organized under the laws of or having its principle place of business as a foreign country"[§611].	Name, principle business address; statement of nature of business; copies of written representational agreements and terms of oral agreements; detailed statement of activity performed; nature and amount of contributions, income, money, or things of value received; and summary of money spent [§612(a)].	Every 6 months, within 30 days of the end of each filing period [§612(b)].	Statement filed under oath [§612(c)]. Required to keep books of accounts and other records [§615]. Attorney General is required to make statements public over the internet in a searchable, sortable, and downloadable manner without charge [§616(d)(1)].[d]
Regulation of Lobbying Act (RLA) P.L. 79-601, title III,60 Stat. 839, August 2, 1946	"[A]ny persons" who are paid to accomplish "the passage or defeat of any legislation" or to "influence, directly or indirectly, the passage or defeat of any legislation" by Congress [§307].[a]	Name and address of contributors; name and address of expense recipients; and "total sum of expenditure made ...during the calendar year" [§305(a)].	Between the 1st and 10th day of each calendar quarter [§305(a)].	Information published in the *Congressional Record* by the Clerk of the House and Secretary of the Senate [§308(b)]. Reports made under oath [§309]. Records preserved for two years from date of filing [§306(b)].

Table 1. (Continued)

	Registration of Whom	Disclosure of What	How Often	How Public
Lobbying Disclosure Act (LDA) P.L. 104-65, 109 Stat. 691,December 19, 1995 2 U.S.C. §§1601-1614	Lobbyists; "any individual who is employed or retained by a client for financial or other compensation for services that include more than one lobbying contact, other than an individual whose lobbying activities constitute less than 20 percent of the time engaged in services provided by such individual client over a six-month period" [§1602(10)].	*Registration* Information on registrant and information on client [§1603(b)]. *Disclosure* Name of registrant; changes or updates to registration information; specific issues for which contact was made; statement of agencies or House of Congress lobbied;estimate of lobbying income or expenses [§1604(b)].	*Registration* Within 45 days of making a lobbying contact or being first employed [§1603(a)]. *Disclosure* Every six months [§1604(a)].	Clerk of the House and Secretary of the Senate make registration and disclosure statements available for public inspection [§1605(4)].

	Registration of Whom	Disclosure of What	How Often	How Public
Honest Leadership and Open Government Act (HLOGA) P.L. 110-81, title II,121 Stat. 741,September 14, 2007 2 U.S.C. §§1601-1614	Added certain coalitions and associations to required filers [§1603(b)(3)].[b]	Created semiannual report on certain campaign contributions [§1604(d)]. Created disclosure of bundled contributions under the Federal Election Campaign Act of 1974 [§204; 2 U.S.C. §434].	*Disclosure*[c] Every 3 months [§1604(a)].	Registration and disclosure reports are required to be available over the internet, "without a fee or other access charge, in a searchable, sortable, and downloadable manner" [§1605].

Source: CRS Summary and Analysis of Foreign Agents Registration Act, Regulation of Lobbying Act, Lobbying Disclosure Act, and Honest Leadership and Open Government Act.

Notes:

[a] A person is defined to include an "individual, partnership, committee, association, corporation, and any other organization or group of persons" [P.L. 79-601, §302(c), 60 Stat. 840, August 2, 1946].

[b] Coalitions and associations are required to register if they (1) "contribute more than $5,000 to the registrant or the client in the quarterly period to fund lobbying ... " and (2) "actively participates in the planning, supervision, or control of such lobbying activities" [§207(a)(1)].

[c] Registration timeline requirements under the Lobbying Disclosure Act were not amended by the Honest Leadership and Open Government Act.

[d] The provision requiring the Attorney General to publish statements on the internet was added by P.L. 110- 81, §212(b), 121 Stat. 749, September 14, 2007.

Examining the enactment of FARA, RLA, LDA, and HLOGA provides insight into why the laws were passed and which factors—practice or perception—might have caused the need for new legislation. The RLA, FARA, the LDA, and HLOGA were all partly responses to an altered *perception* about what lobbyists should or should not be doing. For FARA, the law was a response to anti-German sentiment and fears of European and Asian influence on American foreign policy. The RLA responded to the belief that lobbyists had undue influence over governmental decision making, and the LDA provided a shift toward further requirements that lobbyists' activities be disclosed on a recurring basis. For HLOGA, the amendments to the LDA were partly in response to the Abramoff scandal.

Data on Lobbying Trends

When the LDA was enacted, it required the Clerk of the House and the Secretary of the Senate to make registration and disclosure statements available to the public. Since at least 1999, that data has been available online.[84] Using this data, a picture of the lobbying landscape emerges. The LDA data provides a window into the number of newly registered lobbyists and the number of disclosure statements filed. While the data can provide information on these indicators of lobbying behavior, it does not provide a complete picture of the number of lobbyists or lobbying activity.

This section provides insight into the historic and current landscape of lobbying through the analysis of data on registration and disclosure under the LDA (pre-2007) and under the HLOGA amendments (2008-present). LDA data are used to evaluate the number of registration and disclosures between 1999 (the first year that data is available) and 2007. HLOGA data are then used to consider the impact of the 2007 amendments to LDA and how registration and disclosure has changed over time.

Lobbyists Registration and Disclosure, Pre-2007

The number of registered lobbyists has changed over time. For example, in 1967, under the RLA, the media reported that "[f]rom a peak of 312 organizations reporting $10.3 million in lobbying expenses in 1950, the figures dropped to 225 groups spending $4.3 million in 1954, the year of the *Harriss* decision.... In 1966, 296 organizations reported spending a total of $4.7

million" in nominal dollars.[85] While comprehensive data on the number of lobbyists who registered under the RLA are not available, data are available for more recent filings. **Figure 1** shows the number of new registrations by lobbyists under the LDA between 1999 and 2007.

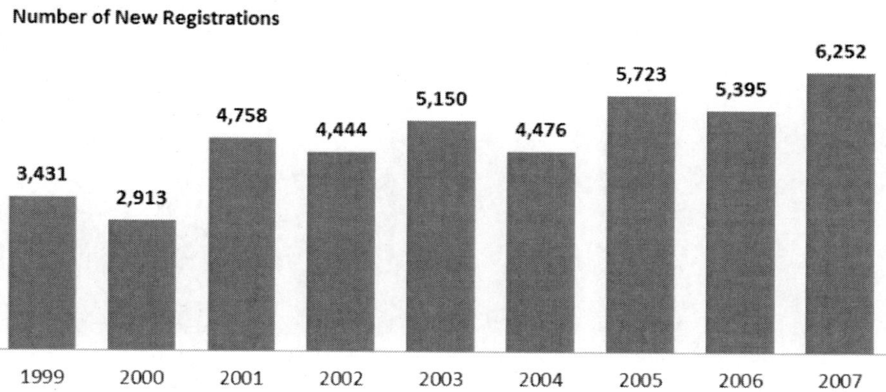

Source: CRS analysis of data from the Secretary of the Senate.

Figure 1. New Lobbyist Registration Under LDA, 1999-2007.

As shown in **Figure 1**, the number of new lobbyist registrations shows a generally upward trend between 1999 and 2007. While some years show declines in new registrations (e.g., even-numbered years), these declines generally coincide with election years and the potential need for lobbying firms and corporations that employ lobbyists to hire (or fire) individuals according to shifts in party control of Congress or the executive branch or shifts in the issue agenda as a result of elections.

Similar to an examination of registration and termination, Figure 2 shows the number of disclosure reports (i.e., quarterly filings that provide basic information on the lobbyist or lobbying firm, a list of specific issues covered, branch of government contacted, name of client, and estimates of lobbying expenditures or income) filed between 2001 and 2007.

As shown in Figure 2, the number of disclosure reports rose steadily between 2001 and 2007, peaking at almost 20,000 disclosures filed in the mid-year reporting period of 2007. Taken together, the trends in Figure 1 and Figure 2 show a general increase in the number of individuals who were required to register and their disclosures under the LDA.

Data from the LDA era can be compared to limited data available under the RLA. In January 1975, for example, 1,772 active lobbyists were registered with the Secretary of the Senate.[86] The higher numbers of lobbyist registration under LDA could be evidence of either more effective disclosure requirements or additional lobbying activity.

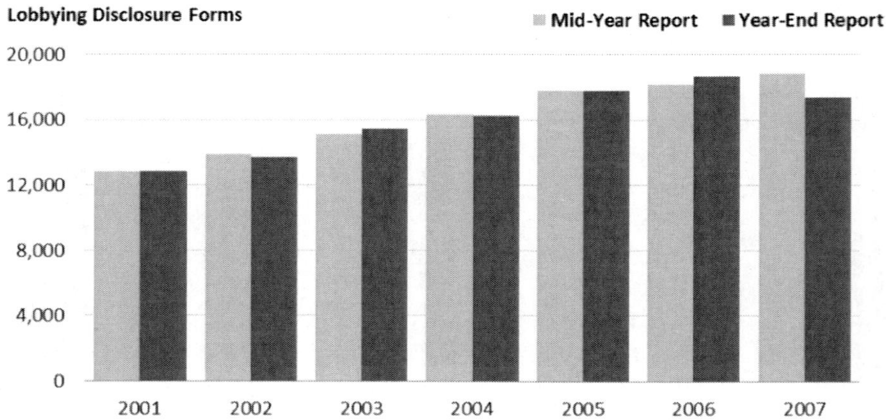

Source: CRS analysis of data from U.S. Congress, Clerk of the House of Representatives, *Lobbying Disclosure*, at https://lobbyingdisclosure.house.gov.

Figure 2. Number of Lobbyists Disclosure Forms Filed, 2001-2007.

Lobbyist Registration and Disclosure, 2007-Present

With the enactment of HLOGA in 2007, registration continued to be required within 45 days "after a lobbyist makes a lobbying contact or is employed or retained to make a lobbying contact."[87] As Figure 3 shows, the number of new lobbyists registered initially increased under HLOGA.

The number of new registration increased in 2009, before declining between 2010 and 2014. In 2009, a record 6,509 new lobbyists were registered. This number may reflect a number of trends that stem from change in party control of the White House and Congress. For example, in 2006 the majority party in the House changed from a Republican majority to a Democratic majority, in 2009, the president changed from a Republican to a Democrat, which unified control of the White House and Congress under a single political party. Additionally, changes in registration numbers could reflect the continued implementation of HLOGA.

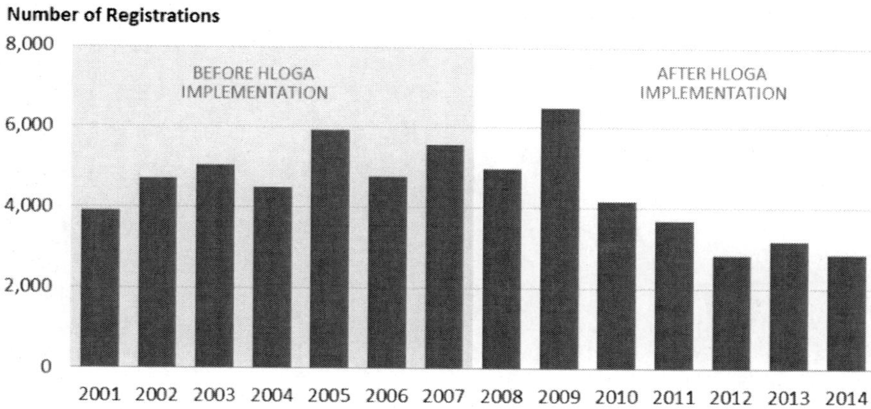

Source: CRS analysis of Clerk of the House data.

Figure 3. New Lobbyist Registration, 2001-2014.

Further, several media reports suggested a link between declines in the number of lobbyists and the earmark ban that was adopted at the beginning of the 112th Congress (2011-2012).[88] Support for the link between the earmark ban and the decline in the number of registered lobbyists, however, has not been found through academic studies. That the decline in lobbyists began in 2009, before the 2011 earmark ban, points to other possible reasons as the most likely cause of the decline in registered lobbyists.[89]

HLOGA provides an opportunity to evaluate disclosure trends on a quarterly, instead of semiannual, basis. Figure 4 shows the number of disclosure filings per quarter has declined since the enactment of HLOGA for 2008. The number of disclosure filings provides a different way to examine lobbying data. Instead of examining the number of new registrants per year, disclosure statements allow an analysis of lobbying activity through an evaluation of the number of disclosure forms filed.

A lobbyist or lobby firm files a report regardless of whether any lobbying activity occurred during the quarterly period. If no lobbying activities occurred in a particular quarter, the firm can indicate that on the form.[90] The decline in disclosure reports, therefore, does not necessarily reflect a decrease in filing by active lobbyists. Instead, it could reflect a general decline in the number of new lobbyists registering under the LDA in combination with the number of lobbyists who might have terminated their registration in any given quarterly period.

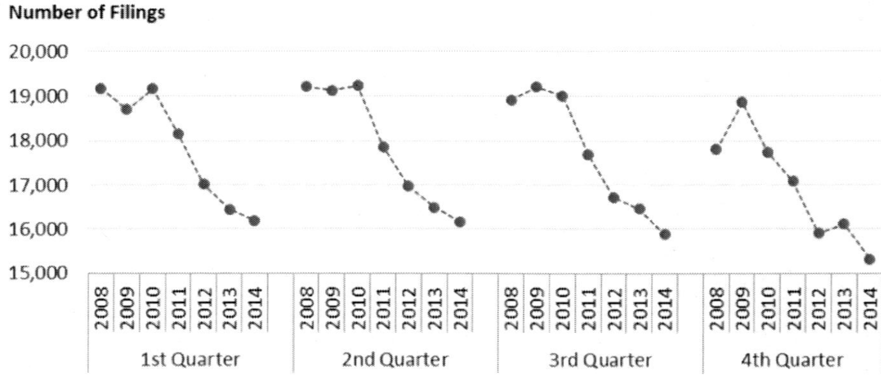

Source: CRS analysis of Clerk of the House data.

Figure 4. Quarterly Disclosure Filing Under HLOGA, 2008-2014.

CONTEMPORARY LOBBYING OBSERVATIONS

An examination of contemporary lobbying reveals that scholars, think tanks, and legislators are still thinking about registration and disclosure, often within the context of three current trends. These are shadow lobbying, grassroots lobbying, and the revolving door.

Shadow Lobbying

In June 2014, the Office of Congressional Ethics (OCE)[91]—an independent, non-partisan entity constituted by the House of Representatives and charged with review of allegations of misconduct by Members of the House, House officers, and House staff—reported that it had referred an "entity to the U.S. Attorney's Office for the District of Columbia for failure to register under the Lobbying Disclosure Act."[92] According to news reports of the referral, this was the first time a referral for violation of the LDA's registration provisions has occurred.[93] Further, the referral highlighted that the U.S. Attorney's Office for the District of Columbia has prosecuted only a handful of LDA cases,[94] although that number has increased over the past several years.[95]

What made OCE's referral for non-compliance with the LDA so remarkable is that it raised the issue of individuals who engage in lobbying activities, but do not register under the LDA to the forefront. Labeled as "shadow lobbyists," by the scholarly community, the OCE has provided the first government entity acknowledgement that certain individuals might be lobbying, but not registering or disclosing their activities to the Clerk of the House and the Secretary of the Senate.

An individual might be considered a "shadow lobbyist" if they engages in some lobbying activities, but do not believe they strictly meet all of the requirements for registration as a lobbyist—makes more than one lobbying contact per quarter, is compensated for making contacts with covered officials, and spends more than 20% of his or her time on lobbying activities. As described by political scientist Timothy LaPira, a shadow lobbyist is

> ...any professional who is paid to challenge or defend the policy status quo, to subsidize [sic] policymakers with information, or to closely monitor intricate policy and political developments that are not readily available to the public—or those who offer expertise, knowledge, and access in support of these activities—yet who do not register as lobbyists.[96]

Individuals might choose not to register under the LDA for several reasons. First, the definition of lobbying requires that a lobbyist must register when they meet all three parts of the statutory definition—one contact per quarter, receive compensation, and 20% of time spent on lobbying activities. Individuals self-report whether or not they meet these criteria.

Second, as discussed below under "Revolving Door," former high-ranking government officials (including Members of Congress) and senior staff are prohibited from engaging in certain representational activities, such as lobbying or advocacy directed to influence current federal officials for a certain period of time.[97] These restrictions last for either one or two years, depending on whether the former official worked in the executive, the House, or the Senate. Subsequently, former government officials often do not qualify as statutory lobbyists since they are prohibited from making advocacy contacts during their "cooling off" period, even if they support the lobbying of others.

Identifying the number of individuals who might be considered shadow lobbyists has been inexact for two reasons. First, some numbers of registered lobbyists do not report activity in any given quarterly period, but they may continue to lobby without making the appropriate disclosures.[98] These individuals could be spending less than 20% of their time lobbying, make no contacts, or receive no compensation in a quarterly period. Some, however, suggest that non-reporting of activities by registered lobbyists is a purposeful attempt to skirt the LDA.[99]

Second, some individuals who work as "strategic policy advisors" or consultants seemingly engage in lobbying activities but never register under the LDA. Some studies have examined former Members of Congress who fit this description and concluded that much of the work done by these individuals should be considered lobbying, thus requiring registration under the LDA.[100] Others take issue with this position and believe that government relations are fundamentally different than lobbying.[101]

Whether these individuals meet the statutory definition of a lobbyist is an open question. Since the LDA definition of lobbying requires self-reporting of time spent engaged in lobbying activities and the number of lobbying contacts made, it is conceivable that individuals could not need to register. Conversely, because of the civil and criminal penalties potentially associated with non-compliance, some individuals may preemptively register to avoid even the possible perception of impropriety.

Estimating the number of shadow lobbyists is difficult. One approach to determining the number of shadow lobbyists examined the employment of formerly registered lobbyists.[102] Another study took a sample of former lobbyists and used public and proprietary directories, websites, and social networks to identify current employment. For this study, when current employment matched the definition of lobbying, the individual was categorized as a lobbyist regardless of whether he or she was actually registered under the LDA.[103]

If individuals are choosing not to register under the LDA and they continue to engage in lobbying activities, the decline in the number of registered lobbyists and the number of disclosure forms filed provides possible but not conclusive evidence that the number of shadow lobbyists is increasing. Figure 5 shows an estimate of the total number of lobbyists between 1998 and 2012.

As Figure 5 shows, the estimated number of lobbyists has declined since the enactment of HLOGA in December 2007 and the provision went into effect in January 2008.[104] The decline could be explained in several ways. First, the decrease in registered lobbyists could reflect a possible increase in the number of shadow lobbyists. In this scenario, HLOGA's increased disclosure requirements, including provisions requiring lobbyists to disclose campaign contributions, may have created an incentive for lobbyists to deregister to possibly avoid the filings.[105] Second, deregistration combined with a decrease in new registrations (see Figure 3) could reflect a policy shift by President Barack Obama to prohibit lobbyists from serving on federal advisory committees.[106] Third, the decline in registration could reflect a change in presidential administration from President George W. Bush to President Obama. Lobbying firms may have shifted resources as a result of the policy differences and attitude toward lobbyists between the Presidents. Fourth, the economic realities of the 2008-2009 recession could have resulted in less demand for lobbyists and, therefore, a reduction in registrations.

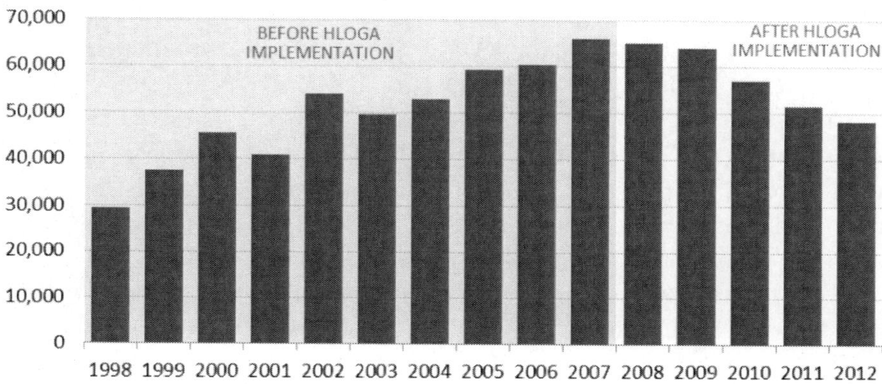

Source: George H.W. Bush School of Government and Public Service at Texas A&M and CRS analysis of data provided by Dr. Tim LaPira, James Madison University.

Figure 5. Estimated Total Number of Lobbyists, 1998-2012.

As the number of registered lobbyists has declined, a change in practice and perception could be taking place. Because individuals who might have previously registered under the LDA are perhaps choosing not to, a change in the practice of who registers might be occurring. Additionally, as the number of registered lobbyists has declined, the perception of who ought to be classified as a lobbyist could be changing to include individuals or activities that previously might not have been considered advocacy or lobbying, like those who primarily work with grassroots organizations. Additionally, what might have been considered lobbying previously might not be considered lobbying today (or vice versa).

Grassroots Lobbying

Grassroots lobbying is the attempt to persuade policymakers by influencing public opinion and motivating citizens to take action, often by asking them to contact their Representatives and Senators.[107] Grassroots lobbying traditionally includes a variety of actors, including individual citizens, corporations, and advocacy groups. According to one observer, grassroots lobbying is used for a wide range of issues, but most often for matters that "involve a great departure from the status quo, and draw the most attention."[108]

Grassroots lobbying is differentiated from other forms of lobbying by the methods deployed. Instead of using professionals to contact decisionmakers directly, grassroots lobbying uses various strategies to get constituents to make contact. These strategies include having constituents call, write letters, make personal visits, protest, or send emails that advocacy groups help craft.[109] Grassroots lobbying can show Representatives and Senators that constituents "are willing to take ... action to inform their legislators about their preferences on an issue."[110] While some grassroots strategies have little or no cost (e.g., email), others may have significant cost of time and money (e.g., traveling to participate in a Capitol Hill day with a professional association).

With few exceptions, grassroots lobbying remains unregulated.[111] Past attempts have been made to regulate grassroots lobbying. For example, as introduced, the Senate version of HLOGA (S. 1, 110th Congress), contained a provision that would have required grassroots lobbying activities to be registered with and disclosed under the LDA. Introduced as Section 220 of HLOGA, grassroots lobbying would have been defined as "the voluntary efforts of members of the general public to communicate their own views on an issue to Federal officials or to encourage other members of the general public to do the same."[112] Subsequently, firms that promoted grassroots lobbying would have had to register pursuant to LDA provisions within 45 days of being "retained by a client to engage in paid efforts to stimulate grassroots lobbying.... "[113] Following registration, firms would have had to disclose estimates of income or expenses related to their grassroots efforts.[114]

According to one Senator, Section 220 was initially drafted to deal with what some called "astroturf" lobbying:

> An astroturf lobbyist is someone who gets paid, presumably by a large organization—a labor union, a corporation, a trade association, whatever it might be—to pretend there is a groundswell of grassroots support or opposition for or to a particular piece of legislation. So this hired gun, if you will, sends out letters, e-mails, faxes—whatever it is—to stir up phony grassroots support for or against the particular piece of legislation.[115]

Concern over the possible consequences of requiring grassroots lobbyists to register and disclose under the LDA resulted in the introduction of an amendment to delete Section 220 from the bill. In summarizing why the amendment was necessary, a Senator compared requiring the registration of grassroots lobbying efforts with banning constituent contact with Congress.

> Let me stress that again. This legislation says that grassroots lobbying is defined as members of the general public communicating with their Congressman or encouraging others to do the same.
>
> I thought that is what we were all supposed to do. I was taught in civics class in high school that everyone had the right to do that, without being forced to register and report all of their connections if somebody pays for it. Again, the Supreme Court says, constitutional protection of lobbying is not in the least diminished by the fact that it may be performed for others for a fee. But if you mess up your forms, if you don't file them on time, if somehow they are confusing to you and you have contacted your neighbors or have purchased a mailing list ... you are on the hook for $200,000, as the bill currently stands.[116]

In defense of Section 220, another Senator laid out the case for disclosure as a way to understand how money was being spent to fund grassroots campaigns, not to discourage citizens from contacting Congress:

> This legislation simply requires disclosure of the amount of money spent on grassroots lobbying when it is conducted by professional organizations. The opponents of this measure would have us believe we are trying to amend the first amendment. That is not true. Our Senate phones are often jammed with callers expressing their points of view and all giving the exact same message. That comes from somewhere, is paid for by somebody and is part of an organized effort, and the public and the Members have a right to know who is paying and how much.[117]

After debate, the Senate agreed to the amendment and removed Section 220 from HLOGA.[118]

The debate over the possible regulation of grassroots lobbying highlights the complexity in balancing the disclosure of lobbying activities and First Amendment protections of the right to petition. Recent studies on lobbying have highlighted the potential difficulty in understanding the scope of grassroots lobbying because groups that prompt such lobbying are not required to register or disclosure under the LDA.[119] For example, past studies have indicated "that 56% of interest groups regularly mobilize group members and an additional 38% of groups occasionally mobilize members,"[120] and the use of grassroots tactics, such as email, can have a large influence on legislative behavior.[121]

Differentiating the mobilization of members by an interest group from corporate use of grassroots tactics (i.e., "astroturf" lobbying) is also increasingly difficult. Sociologist Edward Walker argues that corporations are using grassroots tools to influence policy precisely because politicians listen to constituents in a different way than they listen to corporate lobbyists.[122] In fact, he recognizes that while "organized interests have always sought to facilitate popular participation through offering publics various types of incentives to get involved ... new communications technologies, professional practices for popular mobilization, and a changed field of advocacy organizations have combined to make it much easier for elites to recruit citizen activists."[123]

Groups have encouraged constituents to contact Members of Congress since before the ratification of the Constitution.[124] Modern technology, however, has enabled groups and corporations to engage individual citizens more effectively and more efficiently. Additionally, the number of opportunities for groups to ask individuals to write, email, call, or contact their Member of Congress through social media platforms has increased. Subsequently, these increased contact opportunities could result in a shift in both practice and perception.

As new platforms and technologies make communications with Members easier and less expensive, constituents may choose to engage Members of Congress more frequently—thus changing the practice of how Members interact with constituents. This could increase the number of incoming letters, emails, and social media interactions exponentially, thus potentially taxing the limited resources of Representatives and Senators. Further, the potential for increased constituent communication could change Member-constituent interaction. If Members perceive that grassroots organizations are influencing constituent communications, it is possible that certain mass communications could be treated differently by Members than individualized letters, email, or social media postings. This change in treatment could serve to marginalize certain constituent voices that have traditionally been activated by interest groups employing grassroots strategies.

Requiring grassroots lobbying firms to register and disclose activities, however, could have an effect on the volume of grassroots lobbying. If groups were required to register and disclose grassroots activities and they did not want to do so, they might face three choices: they could not comply with the law, they could stop using grassroots strategies to engage the general public, or they could alter their activities short of ceasing grassroots lobbying.

Should Congress desire that grassroots firms disclose activities, current LDA definitions of lobbying activities and the type of activities that trigger registration and disclosure would likely need to be amended. Amendments might focus on requiring grassroots organization to disclose income and expenses or the issue a grassroots campaign addresses. Additionally, an amendment could require that the grassroots firm disclose their client. Requiring the disclosure of the client might mirror current FARA requirements that foreign agents disclose the foreign government or entity with which they have a contract. Making any amendments to the current LDA to address grassroots, however, could make grassroots efforts more difficult.

Revolving Door

On a regular basis, federal employees leave the government for private sector employment, while the government also hires former private sector employees for government jobs. Often called the "revolving door," this practice can include individuals in all professions, ranging from career bureaucrats and congressional staff, to Members of Congress, and individuals appointed to executive branch positions by the President with the advice and consent of the Senate. Because personal networks and connections are often considered the highest form of currency in Washington, former Members of Congress, executive branch officials, and high-ranking staff connections and knowledge of the system are valuable to many outside of government.[125]

Revolving door provisions were initially enacted for several purposes, including the following:

- protecting against the use of proprietary information by former employees who might trade insider knowledge to the potential detriment of public interest;[126]
- limiting the potential influence that the allure of future employment might have on a federal employee when dealing with prospective private clients or future employers while still with the government;[127] and
- avoiding "the appearance of making unfair use of Government employment and affiliations," for private gain.[128]

Several laws govern the movement of federal employees from the government to the private sector and vice versa. Most prominently, 18 U.S.C. §207 provides a series of post-employment restrictions on "representational" activities for executive branch personnel when they leave government service, including

- a lifetime ban on "switching sides" on a matter involving specific parties on which any executive branch employee had worked personally and substantially while with the government;
- a two-year ban on "switching sides" on a somewhat broader range of matters which were under the employee's official responsibility;
- a one-year restriction on assisting others on certain trade or treaty negotiations;
- a one-year "cooling off" period for certain "senior" officials barring representational communications before their former departments or agencies;
- a two-year "cooling off" period for "very senior" officials barring representational communications to and attempts to influence certain other high ranking officials in the entire executive branch of government; and
- a one-year ban on certain officials in performing some representational or advisory activities for foreign governments or foreign political parties.[129]

In Congress, post-employment restrictions are applied by the House and Senate respectively. In the House, Members and senior staff are subject to a one-year "cooling off" period, during which they cannot make lobbying contact with Representatives, Senators, or congressional staff.[130] In the Senate, a two-year ban on lobbying is in place. During this time, Senators cannot make lobbying contacts with anyone in Congress, as well as legislative branch employees. For senior Senate staff, a one-year "cooling off" period is in place.[131]

In addition to statutory revolving door restrictions, President Obama has instituted an ethics pledge (see Appendix for full text) that restricts registered lobbyists from serving in his Administration without receiving a waiver from the Office of Management and Budget (OMB).[132] Additionally, the pledge puts further restrictions on executive branch employees preventing them from using the revolving door for immediate employment outside government that requires advocacy on issues covered during federal employment.[133]

Discussion of whether the revolving door is positive or negative center around whether former government employees, when they switch jobs, have an inherent or perceived conflict of interest. Though lobbying legislation often treats the revolving door as a negative trend, the movement of individuals between the government and private sector may also present multiple potential benefits. Proponents of the revolving door, for example, observe that the promise of future private-sector employment could potentially improve the quality of candidates applying for government jobs.[134] Further, direct connections to government officials are important, but a close relationship is not necessarily what drives lobbying. While some believe that government employees contemplating a move to the private sector will be friendly to industry interests at the expense of the public interest, studies have shown that regulators instead may engage in more aggressive actions against industry and do not favor industry, regardless of their job prospects.[135]

Additionally, the flow of personnel between the public and private sectors may increase the knowledge base of both sectors.

Critics of the revolving door and the movement of employees between the government and private sectors advocate for longer "cooling off" periods and stronger restrictions related to conflict of interest. Additionally, critics often assert that the revolving door has negative effects for the transparency and efficiency of government. These critics see existing bias between those in government and their connections with lobbying firms and the potential for those connections to be exploited when the individual is employed by the private sector.[136]

Additional criticism of the revolving door often focuses on the worth of a former government employee over time. With the possible exception of former Members of Congress or Cabinet officials, research has shown that a majority of revenue generated by private lobbying firms was directly attributable to employees with previous government experience.[137] Another study found that "'who you know' rather than 'what you know' drives a good proportion of lobbying revenues."[138] The "who you know" observation is further bolstered by a study that showed that lobbyists with experience in the office of a U.S. Senator suffer a 24% drop in generated revenue when that Senator leaves office. The effect for the former staffer is immediate, discontinuous around the exit period, and long-lasting.[139]

Making any adjustments to revolving door restrictions might be motivated by a change in perception. When a Member of Congress resigns or a senior staffer leaves the government to take a job as a lobbyist or elsewhere in the private sector, questions often arise as to whether these individuals have a conflict of interest if they go to work on issues they "covered" for the federal government. This arguably results in a change of perception about the role that Members of Congress and senior staff should play both inside and outside of government and raises concern about the potential for impropriety by former officials once they have left the government. As individuals depart the government for the private sector, they take with them knowledge of the legislative or regulatory process that can be valuable for non-governmental interests seeking to influence government action.

Additionally, adjustments to the revolving door might lead others to favor fewer restrictions on the flow of personal between the public and private sectors. The might lead to the acknowledgement that the federal government and private sector can both benefit when employees move between sectors.

OPTIONS FOR CONGRESSIONAL ACTION

The practice and perception of lobbying continues to evolve. New technologies, including social media,[140] have provided lobbyists with new ways to contact decisionmakers and were not contemplated when the HLOGA was enacted in 2007. Should a desire for change occur, Congress may wish to consider the appropriate balance between desired restrictions and the protection of the first amendment's right to petition.

Current laws focus on the registration of lobbyists, the disclosure of lobbying activities, and regulating how federal officials and employees use the revolving door. Additionally, lobbying law provides specific penalties for violation of the LDA and gives administrative authority to the Clerk of the House and the Secretary of the Senate and enforcement authority to the Department of Justice (DOJ). Should Congress want to consider amending the current lobbying laws to address the revolving door, shadow lobbying, or grassroots lobbying, several options could exist. These might include amending the definition of lobbying, changing disclosure thresholds for registered lobbyists, adjusting resources, and maintaining current lobbying standards. Additionally, Congress could address the revolving door and shadow lobbying through the administration of the LDA.

Change Definition of Lobbying

As discussed earlier under "The Lobbying Disclosure Act of 1995," to be considered a lobbyist, and individual must make at least one lobbying contact in a quarterly period, be compensated, and spend at least 20% of their time on lobbying activities. Should an individual not meet all three of these criteria, by definition he or she is not a lobbyist. Additionally, individuals self-report whether they are lobbyists. As a result, it is possible that someone could not make a lobbying contact, not be compensated, or spend less than 20% of his or her time on lobbying activities and avoid registering and reporting activities. As noted previously, individuals who otherwise appear to be lobbyists but do not fit all three parts of the definition are often labeled as "shadow lobbyists."

Should Congress want to ensure that individuals who are engaged in lobbying activities register with the Clerk of the House and the Secretary of the Senate, adjustments to the statutory definition of lobbying might be considered. Because the definition of a lobbyist has three parts, it might be possible to adjust one, two, or all three of these pieces.

Time Threshold

Amendments could propose raising, lowering, or eliminating the 20% time threshold. Should the threshold be lowered, it is possible that individuals who would not have qualified as lobbyists prior to such an amendment would now be required to register. In some cases, it is possible that individuals who spend comparatively little time on making lobbying contacts (e.g., a senior corporate executive) could have to register under a lower threshold.[141] Should the threshold be raised, it is possible that fewer individuals would report meeting the time needed to be a lobbyist. Finally, if the threshold were eliminated as a criterion, the definition of a lobbyist would depend solely on making contact with a covered official and being paid for one's actions. This change might result in more individuals being required to register. More registrations could provide a clearer picture of who is actually involved in lobbying government. Additional registration requirements, however, could be burdensome for individuals that contact covered officials, are paid for their actions, but spend little time lobbying on issues.

Compensation Requirements

Under current definitions, if an individual is not compensated for any lobbying activities, he or she does not have to register as a lobbyist.[142] Should Congress want to include individuals who lobby on a pro bono basis, the

LDA's monetary requirements could be eliminated as a criterion. This change might increase the number of people who are required to register under the law, thus potentially increasing transparency. Requiring pro bono registration, however, could result in a decrease in individuals willing to lobby on a pro bono basis, thus limiting options for groups or individuals looking for representation in Washington, but who cannot otherwise afford to pay a lobbyist.

Contact Threshold

The LDA currently requires individuals to register if they make more than one lobbying contact in a quarterly period. Since registration is currently required after the first lobbying contact, it might be difficult to draft a provision that would require fewer contacts before registration is required. If Congress required that registration occur on the second (or subsequent) contact, however, the number of registrations may decrease as individuals who only have one contact per quarter would no longer be required to report.

Change Financial Disclosure Thresholds or Reporting Requirements

In addition to requiring registration of lobbying activities, the LDA stipulates that any person (or firm) meeting the definition of a lobbyist must disclose lobbying income (or expenditures). There are currently three ways that a lobbyist or firm can choose to disclose this information. First, the lobbyist or firm can file disclosure reports under the LDA's expense definitions. Under this method, lobbyists or firms must submit, to the best of their ability, an estimate of lobbying income or expenditures (not including grassroots expenses).

The other two reporting methods use the Internal Revenue Code's (IRC's) definition of expenses. These definitions are for groups that are required to report lobbying expenditures under section 6033(b)(8) of the IRC. This includes 501(c) nonprofit entities and 162(e) "for profit organizations (other than lobbying firms) and tax exempt organizations such as trade associations."[143] Under the IRC, organizations must provide information on their lobbying expenses, the amount of lobbying expenses that are nontaxable, the amount spent on grassroots lobbying, and the nontaxable amount spent on grassroots lobbying. Arguably, the variation in lobbying disclosure process allows organizations that are not required to report under the LDA to report under the IRC and avoid the disclosure of grassroots lobbying activities. When lobbyists do not have to disclose certain activities, they may be able to choose how to define their activities to alter the type of information they choose to disclose.

To capture the activities of a larger number of lobbyists and increase transparency, Congress could combine the LDA and IRC criteria and create a uniform reporting system for lobbying income and expenditures. Keeping the LDA's reporting requirements for contact with covered executive and legislative branch officials and maintaining the IRC expenditure reporting standards could create a broader picture of lobbying activities and potentially streamline reporting requirements. Combining LDA and IRC income and expense reporting, however, could require individuals, groups, and firms to report additional financial details to the IRC. Such a requirement could have the effect of forcing individuals, groups, or firms to evaluate how lobbying-related income and expenditures are disclosed. Additionally, it could reduce the disclosure burden on lobbyists and lobbying firms by having fewer reports to file.

The disclosure of additional financial information could also provide additional transparency into how lobbyists and lobbying firms are spending money. Currently, the LDA requires that income and expenditures be rounded to the nearest $10,000 for expenses or income greater than $5,000 for quarterly disclosure reports.[144] This threshold could be adjusted to require more detailed disclosure of income and expenses by eliminating the rounding provision. Lobbyists and lobbying firms, however, might resist more specified reporting as a tacit restriction on their activities. More data could also mean that more oversight and review of the information would be needed.

Alter Lobbying Administration

Historically, enforcement of the LDA has been limited. According to the Government Accountability Office (GAO), "as of February 26, 2015, the USAO [United States Attorney's Office for the District of Columbia] has received 2,308 referrals from both the Secretary of the Senate and the Clerk of the House for failure to comply with LD-2 [quarterly disclosure] reporting requirements cumulatively for filing years 2009 through 2014."[145] Of these 2,308 referrals, about 52 percent (1,196 of 2,308) of the total referrals received are now compliant because lobbying firms either filed their reports or terminated their registrations.... About 48 percent (1,101of 2,308) of referrals are pending further action because USAO was unable to locate the lobbying firm, did not receive a response from the firm, or plans to conduct additional research to determine if it can locate the lobbying firm.[146]

Additionally, according to Lobbyists.info, the publisher of the book *Washington Representatives*, "between 1995 and 2010, only three lawsuits filed by the U.S. Attorney's Office against lobbyists were settled, and since 2010, at least five suits have been filed related to Honest Leadership and Open Government Act (HLOGA) and Foreign Agent Registration Act (FARA) violations."[147]

Should Congress wish to provide additional resources for the enforcement of the LDA, several options exist. These include providing additional monetary or staffing resources to the Clerk of the House and the Secretary of the Senate and the U.S. Attorney's Office for the District of Columbia, combining the administration of FARA and the LDA, and requiring a filing fee for LDA registration and disclosure.

Provide Additional Resources

Additional resources might include more money to hire additional staff for the Clerk of the House and Secretary of the Senate to proactively check registration and disclosure forms for compliance and for the DOJ to hire additional staff to investigate and potentially prosecute noncompliance referrals.

Additional funding to the USAO could allow for additional investigation and prosecution of lobbyists that have not complied with LDA registration or disclosure requirements. As GAO found in its 2014 study, approximately 48% of referrals for noncompliance with the LDA are pending further action. Additional resources could allow the USAO to investigate and potentially prosecute cases more quickly. At this time, however, the USAO does not believe it needs additional resources. It reported to GAO that "it has sufficient resources and authority to enforce LD-2 and LD-203 [campaign contribution disclosure] compliance with LDA. It has one contract paralegal working full time and six attorneys working part time on LDA enforcement issues."[148]

Combine FARA and LDA Administration

Lobbying laws differ for foreign lobbyists (FARA) and domestic lobbyists (LDA). These two laws are administered by two different entities—LDA by the Clerk of the House and the Secretary of the Senate, and FARA by DOJ. To streamline the administration of lobbying registration and disclosure, Congress might consider transferring FARA enforcement to the Clerk of the House and Secretary of the Senate or LDA enforcement to the Department of Justice.

Historically, registration of domestic lobbyists, regardless of whether contact is made with the executive or legislative branch, has been handled by the Clerk of the House and the Secretary of the Senate. Congress could choose to maintain LDA administration with these officers, could add FARA enforcement to their portfolio, or could transfer LDA administration to the Department of Justice. Such a change, however, would likely require additional resources to hire personnel and to realign current LDA or FARA registration and disclosure.

Alternatively, Congress could create a new entity to administer both the LDA and FARA. Creating a new agency could allow a singular focus on lobbying and potentially provide for a holistic view of lobbying registration and disclosure across both domestic and foreign clients and issues, regardless of whether contact is made with the executive or legislative branch. Combining lobbying administration into a new agency, however, could involve significant costs to transfer LDA and FARA data and to hire personnel.

Should Congress merge LDA and FARA enforcement, DOJ would likely retain the right to investigate and potentially prosecute noncompliance. If a combined lobbying administration unit was placed either in Congress or a new (or existing agency), referrals of noncompliance to the USOC would likely still be required for DOJ to potentially take any action.

Institute User or Filing Fees

Should Congress want to provide additional resources for LDA implementation and enforcement, one option could be to implement a user fee to be paid by the lobbyist or lobbying firm. These user fees might be paid at the time of registration, disclosure, or both. User fees are defined by GAO as "a price charged by a governmental agency for a service or product whose distribution it controls," or "any charge collected from recipients of Government goods, services, or other benefits not shared by the public."[149]

User fees can be a generator of revenue that could be used to further finance enforcement activities. In a 1980 report on user fees, GAO summarized user fees as a source of revenue and program support: "User charges can reduce Federal taxes, as well as the costs of certain types of regulation. They are a source of revenue that can partially replace general taxation of individuals and businesses."[150]

Implementing user fees for the LDA could raise additional resources for the Clerk of the House and the Secretary of the Senate, and DOJ for LDA enforcement without having to increase appropriations to these offices.

Implementing an LDA user fee would also more closely align the administration of the LDA with the administration of FARA. Currently, FARA requires a fee for document filing, copies of records, database searches, opinion letters, and copies of annual or semi-annual reports.[151]

If LDA enforcement was supported in whole or in part by user fees, it is possible that user fees might not cover full expenses. If user fees did not cover full expenses, Congress would likely have two choices: authorize additional appropriations or require that the enforcement entity raise money through other associated user fees. For example, while not an exact analogy, a study of the United States Patent and Trademark Office (PTO)—an agency that is a "fully use-fee-funded body"—found that application fees covered one-third of the cost to review applications. Subsequently, the PTO "must subsidize patent examination by assessing fees on other activities."[152]

Some constitutional scholars question when a user fee should be used in lieu of appropriations. For some, when a fundamental, constitutional right is in question—including when nonparticipants might receive benefits from an activity—then they believe that taxes should cover the expenses of implementation of a law.[153] For others, user fees constitute the most direct way for individuals or groups covered by a specific law to pay for its enforcement in a collective way.[154]

Amend Revolving Door Restrictions

Should action to alter revolving door restrictions be desired, several options might exist. These could include extending the "cooling off" period to two years or more, reducing the "cooling off" period, placing a blanket ban on taking certain positions for compensation, and placing a ban on taking certain types of non-governmental positions.

Currently, "cooling off" periods for the House and Senate differ, with a one-year period for Representatives, senior House staff, and senior Senate staff; and two years for Senators.[155] One option might be to make the House and Senate periods equal (at either one or two years) or extend the period further for both chambers. While making the House and Senate "cooling off" period the same length, extending the "cooling off" period to two years could possibly be seen as an unreasonable restriction on post-employment for Members of the House—individuals who serve shorter terms than their Senate counterparts and as a result could return to the private sector faster. Alternatively, Congress could reduce the "cooling off" period. Having a shorter "cooling off period" might increase the talent pool available both inside and outside the government.

Instead of, or in addition to, "cooling off" periods, Congress could enact a blanket restriction on the acceptance of outside employment for the length of the Member's elected term. For example, since a Member of the House is elected to a two-year term,[156] he or she could not resign to take private employment until the end of the term to which they were elected—the beginning of the next Congress.[157] Such a policy might encourage Members to finish their terms before seeking outside employment. Placing post-employment restrictions on Members for the length of the term to which they were elected could have the effect of encouraging Members to remain in office rather than resigning to take a private position. Additionally, placing a restriction on the acceptance of compensation, fees, or other remuneration from any private employment activities would not prohibit Members from resigning to accept presidential appointments or other government jobs.[158]

Several disadvantages to creating such post-employment restrictions on Members potentially exist. First, if the measure prohibited only the acceptance of private compensation, fees, or other remuneration, it is possible that a Member could resign from Congress to take an uncompensated position with any private entity. These positions might be advisory in nature and could carry the promise of future compensation after the end of the former-Member's elected term.

Second, prohibiting private compensation, fees, and other remuneration, does not necessarily account for the potential need of a Member to resign to tend to a family business or other family interests. In these cases, for example, as the result of a death in the family, a Member could feel it necessary to step away from his or her congressional responsibilities to focus on personal matters. Banning the Member from taking compensation from a family business may be seen as overly burdensome.

Finally, prohibiting a Senator from accepting private compensation for the duration of his or her elected term could put an undue burden on the Senator, since he or she is elected to a six-year term and would need to wait until the end of that six-year period to potentially accept a new job. One potential way to equalize the burden across the House and Senate would be to require an intervening election before compensated employment could be accepted. This would require the Senator to wait up to two years before restrictions were lifted.

As a potential alternative to a blanket ban on receiving private compensation, fees, or other remuneration for any private employment activities during that time for which he or she was elected, Congress could ban Members from taking certain positions for the duration of their elected terms. Based on current post-employment restrictions, these positions might be related to advocacy with the potential to interact and influence former colleagues or employees.

Prohibiting Members from resigning their positions to take employment with entities that are required to register under the LDA and FARA could have the effect of making such positions less attractive for a Member until *after* his or her term in office. Current "cooling off" periods, however, already restrict Members from engaging in some of these activities, even if they are not prohibited from accepting the positions for compensation. Prohibiting Members from resigning to take lobbying or foreign agent positions would not necessarily stop them from leaving Congress to accept other non-lobbying positions.

Maintain Current Lobbying Standards

Congress might determine that current lobbying laws are effective or that the potential costs of changes outweigh potential benefits. Instead of amending the LDA or FARA, Congress could continue to use existing law to require lobbyist registration and disclosure. Changes to the LDA or FARA could be made on an as-needed basis through changes to LDA guidance documents issued by the Clerk of the House and Secretary of the Senate,[159] or through the prosecution of lobbying enforcement cases by the Department of Justice.

CONCLUSION

On December 19, 2015, the Lobbying Disclosure Act celebrates its 20th anniversary. Initially enacted to require lobbyists to register and disclose their activities and expenses to Congress, the LDA has been modified over its 20 years to include more frequent disclosure of lobbying activities and the reporting of lobbyists' campaign contributions. Coupled with FARA, the lobbying registration and disclosure regime is designed to protect citizens' right to petition the government, while requiring that those activities be conducted in a transparent manner.

An analysis of the four key lobbying laws enacted since 1946 and scholarly work on lobbying raised three issues that have the potential to cause shifts in lobbying practices and perception: shadow lobbying, grassroots lobbying, and the revolving door. Should Congress wish to address these issues, several options exist.

Specific options include changing the definition of lobbying by amending time thresholds, compensation requirements, or contact thresholds; altering the administration of the LDA by providing additional monetary or staff resources, combining the administration of FARA and LDA either under the Department of Justice, the Clerk of the House and Secretary of the Senate, or a new entity; or instituting user fees or maintaining the current lobbying standards.

Should Congress decide to make changes to the LDA, it will likely be the result of new changes in the practice or perception of lobbying. Whether future amendments to LDA might occur is not known. If history is a guide, however, a shift in the practice or perception of lobbying is likely to occur at some point in the future. At that time, Congress might reevaluate how lobbying registration and disclosure is managed and implemented.

APPENDIX. EXECUTIVE ORDER 13490

Signed by President Obama on January 21, 2009, the order stated:

> Section 1. Ethics Pledge. Every appointee in every executive agency appointed on or after January 20, 2009, shall sign, and upon signing shall be contractually committed to, the following pledge upon becoming an appointee:
>
> "as a condition, and in consideration, of my employment in the United States Government in a position invested with the public trust, I commit myself to the following obligations, which I understand are binding on me and are enforceable under law:
>
> 1) *Lobbyist Gift Ban.* I will not accept gifts from registered lobbyists or lobbying organizations for the duration of my service as an appointee.
> 2) *Revolving Door Ban—All Appointees Entering Government.* I will not for a period of 2 years from the date of my appointment participate in any particular matter involving specific parties that

is directly and substantially related to my former employer or former clients, including regulations and contracts.

3) *Revolving Door Ban—Lobbyists Entering Government.* If I was a registered lobbyist within the 2 years before the date of my appointment, in addition to abiding by the limitations of paragraph 2, I will not for a period of 2 years after the date of my appointment: (a) participate in any particular matter on which I lobbied within the 2 years before the date of my appointment; (b) participate in the specific issue area in which that particular matter falls; or (c)seek or accept employment with any executive agency that I lobbied within the 2 years before the date of my appointment.
4) *Revolving Door Ban—Appointees Leaving Government.* If, upon my departure from the Government, I am covered by the post-employment restrictions on communicating with employees of my former executive agency set forth in section 207(c) of title 18, United States Code, I agree that I will abide by those restrictions for a period of 2 years following the end of my appointment.
5) *Revolving Door Ban—Appointees Leaving Government to Lobby.* In addition to abiding by the limitations of paragraph 4, I also agree, upon leaving Government service, not to lobby any covered executive branch official or non-career Senior Executive Service appointee for the remainder of the Administration.
6) *Employment Qualification Commitment.* I agree that any hiring or other employment decisions I make will be based on the candidate's qualifications, competence, and experience."160

End Notes

[1] P.L. 104-65, 109 Stat. 691, December 19, 1995; 2 U.S.C. §§1601-1614.

[2] U.S. President (Clinton), "Remarks on Signing the Lobbying Disclosure Act of 1995 and an Exchange With Reporters," *Public Papers of the Presidents of the United States: William J. Clinton, 1995*, book 2 (Washington: GPO, 1996), p. 1905, at http://www.gpo.gov/fdsys/pkg/PPP-1995-book2/pdf/PPP-1995-book2-doc-pg1904-2.pdf.

[3] James Madison, "Federalist 10: The Same Subject Continued: The Union as a Safeguard Against Domestic Faction and Insurrection," *Federalist Papers*, at https://www.congress.gov/resources/display/content/The+Federalist+Papers. Madison defined factions as "a number of citizens, whether amounting to a majority or a minority of the whole, who are

united and actuated by some common impulse of passion, or of interest, adversed [sic] to the rights of other citizens, or to the permanent and aggregate interests of the community."

[4] John G. Geer, Wendy J. Schiller, Richard Herrera, and Jeffrey A. Segal, *Gateways to Democracy: An Introduction to American Government, 3rd edition* (Boston, MA: Cengage Learning, 2015), p. 247; and Don Wolfensberger, *Factions and the Public Interest: Federalist No. 10 in 2001*, Wilson Center, Washington, DC, May 18, 2001, at http://www.wilsoncenter.org/sites/default/files/lobbyintro.pdf.

[5] For more information on revolving door provisions, see CRS Report R42728, *Post-Employment, "Revolving Door," Laws for Federal Personnel*, by Jack Maskell. For more information on the House gift rules, see CRS Report RS22566, *Acceptance of Gifts by Members and Employees of the House of Representatives Under New Ethics Rules of the 110th Congress*, by Jack Maskell. For more information on the Senate gift rules, see U.S. Congress, Senate Select Committee on Ethics, "Gifts," at http://www.ethics public/index.cfm/gifts.

[6] In 1628, the English Parliament "forced the King [Charles I] to assent to the Petition of Right. This asked for settlement of Parliament's complaints against the King's non-parliamentary taxation and imprisonments without trial, plus the unlawfulness of martial law and forced billets." For more information see, United Kingdom Parliament, "The Civil War: Charles I and the Petition of Right," *Living Heritage*, at http://www.parliament.uk/about/living-heritage/evolutionofparliament/parliamentaryauthority/civilwar/overview/petition-of-right/.

[7] Stephen A. Higginson, "A Short History of the Right to Petition Government for the Redress of Grievances," *The Yale Law Journal*, vol. 96, no. 1 (November 1986), pp. 142-166; and Norman B. Smith, "'Shall Make No Law Abridging ... ': An Analysis of the Neglected, But Nearly Absolute, Right of Petition," *University of Cincinnati Law Review*, vol. 54, no. 4 (1986), pp. 1153-1197.

[8] In "Federalist 84," Alexander Hamilton expressed his belief that the right to petition was ingrained in the American tradition, and that while likely to be included in a "Bill of Rights" was not included in the Constitution because the Constitution's preamble ('WE, THE PEOPLE of the United States, ...to secure the blessings of liberty to ourselves and our posterity, do ORDAIN and ESTABLISH this Constitution for the United States of American') "is a better recognition of popular rights, than volumes of those aphorisms which make the principle figure in several of our State bills of rights, and which sound much better in a treatise of ethics than in a constitution of government." Alexander Hamilton, "Federalist 84: Certain General and Miscellaneous Objections to the Constitution Considered and Answered," *The Federalist Papers*, at https://www.congress display/content/The+Federalist+Papers.

[9] For more information on the Constitution and the Bill of Rights, see U.S. National Archives and Records Administration, *The Charters of Freedom: "A New World is at Hand,"* at http://www.archives.gov/exhibits/charters/charters.html; and "Bill of Rights (1791)," at http://www.ourdocuments.gov/doc.php?flash=true&doc=13.

[10] U.S. Archives and Record Administration, "Benjamin Franklin Petitions Congress," at http://www.archives.gov/legislative/features/franklin. Debate over Benjamin Franklin's petition was intense. The Constitution (Article 1, Section 9, clause 1), however, prohibited Congress from banning slavery until 1808. It stated: "The Migration or Importation of such Persons as any of the States now existing shall think proper to admit, shall not be prohibited by the Congress prior to the Year one thousand eight hundred and eight ... " U.S. Archives and Record Administration, "Article 1, Section 9, clause 1," *Constitution of the United States*, at http://www.archives.gov/exhibits/charters/constitution_transcript.html.

[11] Joseph J. Ellis, *Founding Brothers: The Revolutionary Generation* (New York: Vintage Book, 2002), p. 81.

[12] Alexis de Tocqueville, "Relationships Between Civil and Political Associations," *Democracy in America*, ed. J.P. Mayer, vol. 2 (Garden City, NY: Anchor Books, 1969 [1831]), pp. 520-524.

[13] 2 U.S.C. §1602 (8)(A).

[14] 2 U.S.C. §1602 (10). The Honest Leadership and Open Government Act of 2007 amended the original LDA definition of a lobbyist to require contact over a three-month instead of a six-month period. For the original language, see P.L. 104-65, 109 Stat. 695, December 19, 1995.

[15] For a list of covered legislative branch and executive branch officials, see 2 U.S.C. §1602 (3) and (4); and footnotes 17 and 18.

[16] Anthony J. Nownes, *Total Lobbying: What Lobbyists Want (and How They Try to Get It)* (New York: Cambridge University Press, 2006), pp. 16-22.

[17] 2 U.S.C. §1602 (4). Covered legislative branch officials include

(A) a Member of Congress; (B) an elected officer of either House of Congress; (C) any employee of, or any other individual functioning in the capacity of an employee of (i) a Member of Congress; (ii) a committee of either House of Congress; (iii) the leadership staff of the House of Representatives or the leadership staff of the Senate; (iv) a joint committee of Congress; and (v) a working group or caucus organized to provide legislative services or other assistance to Members of Congress; and (D) any other legislative branch employee serving in a position described under section 109(13) of the Ethics in Government Act of 1978 (5 U.S.C. App.).

[18] 2 U.S.C. §1602 (3). Covered executive branch officials include

(A) the President; (B) the Vice President; (C) any officer or employee, or any other individual functioning in the capacity of such an officer or employee, in the Executive Office of the President; (D) any officer or employee serving in a position in level I, II, III, IV, or V of the Executive Schedule, as designated by statute or Executive order; (E) any member of the uniformed services whose pay grade is at or above O–7 under section 201 of title 37; and (F) any officer or employee serving in a position of a confidential, policy-determining, policy-making, or policy-advocating character described in section 7511(b)(2)(B) of title 5.

[19] Nownes, *Total Lobbying*, p. 28.

[20] Rogan Kersh, "The Well-Informed Lobbyist: Information and Interest Group Lobbying," in *Interest Group Politics*, ed. Allan J. Cigler and Burdett A. Loomis, 7th ed. (Washington, DC: CQ Press, 2007), pp. 389-411.

[21] Robert C. Byrd, "Lobbyists," *The Senate, 1789-1989: Addresses on the History of the United States Senate*, edited by Wendy Wolff, 100th Cong., 1st sess., S.Doc. 100-20 (Washington: GPO, 1991), p. 501.

[22] Harmon Zeigler, "The Effects of Lobbying: A Comparative Assessment," *Western Political Quarterly*, vol. 22, no. 1 (March 1969), pp. 126-127. Lobbyists who convey information, however, often do so to supporters, not to opponents or the undecided.

[23] Zeigler, "The Effects of Lobbying: A Comparative Assessment," p. 127.

[24] Byrd, "Lobbyists," p. 492.

[25] Richard L. Hall and Alan V. Deardorff, "Lobbying as Legislative Subsidy," *American Political Science Review*, vol. 100, no. 1 (February 2006), p. 71.

[26] John R. Wright, *Interest Groups and Congress: Lobbying, Contributions, and Influence* (Boston: Allyn and Bacon, 1996), pp. 69-71.

[27] For example, see Martha A. Derthick, *Up in Smoke: From Legislation to Litigation in Tobacco Politics*, 2nd ed. (Washington: CQ Press, 2005), pp. 138-142; and Daniel E. Bergan, "Does Grassroots Lobbying Work? A Field Experiment Measuring the Effects of an e-Mail Lobbying Campaign on Legislative Behavior," *American Politics Research*, vol. 37, no. 2 (March 2009), pp. 327-352.

[28] Linda L. Fowler and Ronald G. Shaiko, "The Grass Roots Connection: Environmental Activists and Senate Roll Calls," *American Journal of Political Science*, vol. 31, no. 3 (August 1987), pp. 484-510.

[29] Byrd, "Lobbyists," p. 502.

[30] Nicholas W. Allard, "Lobbying Is an Honorable Profession: The Right to Petition and the Competition to be Right," *Stanford Law and Policy Review*, vol. 19, no 1 (January 2008), pp. 23-68.

[31] John W. Kingdon, *Agendas, Alternatives, and Public Policies, 2nd edition* (New York: Harper Collins, 1995).

[32] For more information on concerns about Nazi and other subversive groups influencing American policy, see Francis R. O'Hara, "The Foreign Agents Registration Act—The Spotlight of Pitiless Publicity," *Villianova Law Review*, vol. 10, no. 2 (Spring 1965), p. 436.

[33] Jack Abramoff was a Washington-based lobbyist who represented Native American tribes on issues related to gambling, among other issues. For more information on Mr. Abramoff, see Kathryn R. L. Rand and Steven Andrew Light, "How Congress Can and Should 'Fix' The Indian Gaming Regulatory Act: Recommendations for Law and Policy Reform," *Virginia Journal of Social Policy & the Law*, vol. 13, no. 3 (Spring 2006), pp. 396-473l; Steven Andrew Light and Kathryn R. L. Rand, "The 'Tribal Loophole' Federal Campaign Finance Law and Tribal Political Participation After Jack Abramoff," *Gaming Law Review*, vol. 10, no. 3 (June 2006), pp. 230-239; and Gregory Koger and Jennifer Nicoll Victor, "Polarized Agents: Campaign Contributions by Lobbyists," *PS: Political Science & Politics*, vol. 42, no. 3 (July 2009), pp. 485-488.

[34] Rep. George Hoar, "Counsel for Cases Before Congress," *Congressional Record*, vol. 4, part 4 (May 20, 1876), p. 3230. Shortly after the House required lobbyists to register with the Clerk of the House, the House and Senate press galleries banned the practice of lobbyists being nominally affiliated with a newspaper to gain access to the House and Senate. According to Senate Historian Donald Ritchie "[t]hese rules defined accreditable correspondents as those whose primary salary came from sending telegraphic dispatches to daily newspapers; barred lobbying by any member of the press gallery; and prohibited all clerks from executive agencies (although not congressional committees)." For more information, see Donald A. Ritchie, *Press Gallery: Congress and the Washington Correspondents* (Cambridge, MA: Harvard University Press, 1991), p. 109; and Byrd, "Lobbyists," p. 501.

[35] The 1876 resolution provided "[t]hat all persons or corporations employing counsel or agents to represent their interests in regard to any measure pending at any time before this House, or any committee thereof, shall cause the name and authority of such counsel or agent to be filed with the Clerk of the House; and no person whose name and authority are not so filed shall appear as counsel or agent before any committee of this House." "Counsel for Cases Before Congress," *Congressional Record*, vol. 4, part 4 (May 20, 1876), p. 3230.

[36] 22 U.S.C. §§611-621.

[37] P.L. 79-601, 60 Stat. 839-842, August 2, 1946. Title III of the Legislative Reorganization Act of 1946 was the "Federal Regulation of Lobbying Act." It was the first law that required persons who lobbied Congress to register with the House of Representatives and the Senate.

[38] P.L. 104-65, 109 Stat. 691, December 19, 1995, as amended by P.L. 105-166, 112 Stat. 38, April 8, 1998; 2 U.S.C. §§1601-1614. The Lobbying Disclosure Act of 1995 repealed the Regulation of Lobbying Act of 1946.

[39] P.L. 110-81, 121 Stat. 739, September 14, 2007. HLOGA amended the 1995 act to further enhance disclosure and reporting requirements for lobbyists and lobbying firms.

[40] 22 U.S.C. §§611-621.

[41] Yuk K. Law, "The Foreign Agents Registration Act: A New Standard for Determining Agency," *Fordham International Law Journal*, vol. 6, no. 2 (1982), p. 365.

[42] U.S. Congress, House Committee on the Judiciary, *Foreign Propaganda*, report to accompany H.R. 1591, 75th Cong., 1st sess., July 28, 1937, H.Rept. 75-1381 (Washington: GPO, 1937), pp. 1-2.

[43] 22 U.S.C. §611(c)(1). Additionally, foreign principals are individuals

who directly or through any other person—(i) engages within the United States in political activities for or in the interests of such foreign principal; (ii) acts within the United States as a public relations counsel, publicity agent, information-service employee or political consultant for or in the interests of such foreign principal; (iii) within the United States solicits, collects, disburses, or dispenses contributions, loans, money, or other things of value for or in the interest of such foreign principal; or (iv) within the United States represents the interests of such foreign principal before any agency or official of the Government of the United States.

[44] 22 U.S.C. §612.

[45] 22 U.S.C. §613.

[46] 22 U.S.C. §614.

[47] 22 U.S.C. §615.

[48] 22 U.S.C. §616.

[49] 22 U.S.C. §618.

[50] Ronald J. Hrebenar and Bryson B. Morgan, *Lobbying in America* (Denver, CO: ABC Clio, 2009), pp. 57-58.

[51] P.L. 79-601, §308(a), 60 Stat. 841, August 2, 1946.

[52] "Improving the Legislative Process: Federal Regulation of Lobbying." *The Yale Law Journal*, vol. 56, no. 2 (January 1947), pp. 306-307.

[53] "Federal Lobbying Act of 1946," *Columbia Law Review*, vol. 47, no 1 (January 1947).

[54] U.S. Congress, Senate Special Committee on the Organization of Congress, *Legislative Reorganization Act of 1946*, report to accompany S. 2177, 79th Cong., 2nd sess., May 31, 1946, S.Rept. 79-1400 (Washington: GPO, 1946), p. 4.

[55] Ibid., p. 5. The committee also provided a detailed list of items the RLA would not cover. These included,

First. It does not curtail the right of free speech or freedom of the press or the right to petition. Second. It has no application to the publishers of newspapers, magazines, or other publications, acting in the regular course of business. Third. It has no application to persons who appear openly and frankly before the committees of Congress and engage in no other activities to influence legislation. Fourth. It does not require any reports of any persons or organizations now required to report under the provisions of the present Corrupt Practices Act. Fifth. It does not apply in any manner to person who appear voluntarily without compensation. Sixth. It does not apply to organizations formed for other purposes who efforts to influence legislation are merely incidental to the purposes for which formed (pp. 26-27).

[56] U.S. General Accounting Office, *The Federal Regulation of Lobbying Act—Difficulties in Enforcement and Administration*, GGD-75-79, April 2, 1975, p. 1, at http://www.gao.gov/assets/120/113142.pdf#page=7.

[57] For example, see Kathryn Allamong Jacob, *King of the Lobby: The Life and Times of Sam Ward Man-AboutWashington in the Gilded Age* (Baltimore, MD: The Johns Hopkins University Press, 2010).

[58] For example, according to a General Accounting Office (GAO) report, "as of January 28, 1975, there were 1,773 active lobbyists registered with the Secretary of the Senate. Of these, 131 lobbyists represented more than one employer while one lobbyist, a law firm, represented 25 employers." U.S. General Accounting Office, *The Federal Regulation of Lobbying Act—Difficulties in Enforcement and Administration*, GGD-75-79, April 2, 1975, p. 7. See also, Testimony of Deputy Comptroller General Robert F. Keller, in U.S. Congress, House, Committee on the Judiciary, Subcommittee on Administrative Law and Governmental Relations, *Examination of Lobbying*, 94th Cong., 1st sess., September 12, 1975, GAO-98176, p. 3, at http://www.gao.gov/assets/100/98176.pdf.

[59] 347 U.S. 612 (1954).

[60] Byrd, "Lobbyists," p. 505 (fn 35).

[61] U.S. General Accounting Office, *The Federal Regulation of Lobbying Act—Difficulties in Enforcement and Administration*, GGD-75-79, April 2, 1975, p. 1, at http://www.gao.gov/assets/120/113142.pdf#page=7.

[62] Byrd, "Lobbyists," p. 506.

[63] U.S. Congress, Senate Committee on Governmental Affairs, *Lobbying Disclosure Act of 1993*, report to accompany S. 349, 103rd Cong., 1st sess., April 1, 1993, S.Rept. 103-37 (Washington: GPO, 1993), p. 3.

[64] Ibid., p. 2. The other laws cited as containing lobbying provisions were the Federal Registration of Lobbying Act of 1946; the Foreign Agents Registration Act; 31 U.S.C. § 1352 (the "Byrd Amendment"); a provision of the Housing and Urban Development (HUD) Reform Act that required lobbyists to disclose contact with the Department of Housing and Urban Development and the Farmers Home Administration; Section 12(i) of the Public Utility Holding Company Act (Federal Energy Regulatory Commission); and 46 U.S.C. §1225 (Federal Maritime Commission).

[65] Sen. Robert Dole, "Lobbying Reform," remarks in the Senate, *Congressional Record*, vol. 141, part 14 (July 25, 1995), p. 20193.

[66] Sen. John Glenn, "Lobbying Disclosure Act of 1995," remarks in the Senate, *Congressional Record*, vol. 141, part 14 (July 24, 1995), p. 20034.

[67] U.S. Congress, House Committee on the Judiciary, *Lobbying Disclosure Act of 1995*, report to accompany H.R. 2564, 104th Cong., 1st sess., H.Rept. 104-339 (Washington: GPO, 1995), p. 2.

[68] "Lobbying Reform," Senate debate, *Congressional Record*, vol. 141, part 14 (July 25, 1995), pp. 20193-20200; and "Lobbying Disclosure Act of 1995," House debate, *Congressional Record*, vol. 141, part 24 (November 29, 1995), pp. 34808-34815.

[69] P.L. 104-65, 109 Stat. 691, December 19, 1995, as amended by P.L. 105-166, 112 Stat. 38, April 8, 1998; 2 U.S.C. §§1601-1614.

[70] For more information on the role of the Clerk of the House and Secretary of the Senate, see CRS Report RL34377, *Lobbying Registration and Disclosure: The Role of the Clerk of the House and the Secretary of the Senate*, by Jacob R. Straus.

[71] Pursuant to 2 U.S.C. §1602(8), a *lobbying contact* means "any oral or written communication (including an electronic communication) to a covered executive branch official or a covered

legislative branch official that is made on behalf of a client with regard to the formulation, modification, or adoption of Federal legislation, ... federal rule, regulation, executive order, the administration or execution of a Federal program or policy ...; or the nomination or confirmation of a person for a position subject to confirmation by the Senate."

[72] William V. Luneburg and A.L. (Lorry) Spitzer, "The Lobbying Disclosure Act of 1995: Scope of Coverage," in *The Lobbying Manual: A Complete Guide to Federal Law Governing Lawyers and Lobbyists*, ed. William V. Luneburg and Thomas M. Susman, 3rd ed. (Chicago: ABA Publishing, 2005), p. 37. Pursuant to 2 U.S.C. §1602(7), "the term 'lobbying activities' means lobbying contacts and efforts in support of such contacts, including preparation and planning activities, research and other background work that is intended, at the time it is performed, for use in contacts, and coordination with the lobbying activities of others."

[73] 2 U.S.C. §1602(3) and (4). Covered executive branch officials are defined as (A) the President; (B) the Vice-President; (C) any officer or employee, or any individual functioning in the capacity of such an officer or employee, in the Executive Office of the President; (D) any officer or employee serving in a position in level I, II, III, IV, or V of the Executive Schedule, as designated by statute or Executive order; (E) any member of the uniformed services whose pay grade is at or above O-7 under 37 U.S.C. §201; and (F) any officer or employee serving in a position of a confidential policy-determining, policy-making, or policy-advocating character described in 5 U.S.C. §7511(b)(2). For more information on executive branch lobbying, see CRS Report R40947, *Lobbying the Executive Branch: Current Practices and Options for Change*, by Jacob R. Straus.

In 1998, technical amendments were made to the LDA (P.L. 105-166, 112 Stat. 38, April 6, 1998). These amendments clarified the definition of covered executive branch officials, more clearly defined what constitutes a lobbying contact, and provided that organizations, whose lobbying activities are limited by their Internal Revenue Code (IRC) non-profit status, could use their tax estimates to report lobbying activities.

[74] Sen. John McCain, "Lobbying Disclosure Act of 1995," *Congressional Record*, vol. 141, part 14 (July 24, 1995), p. 20016.

[75] John W. Kingdon, *Agendas, Alternatives, and Public Policies*, 2nd ed. (New York: Harper Collins, 1995).

[76] P.L. 110-81, 121 Stat. 739, September 14, 2007.

[77] P.L. 110-81, 121 Stat. 735, September 14, 2007. For more information on the Abramoff scandal, see footnote 33.

[78] P.L. 110-81, 121 Stat. 748, September 14, 2007.

[79] The threshold amounts of time and money spent or received to qualify one as a "lobbyist" are adjusted (halved) in P.L. 110-81 to conform to the new quarterly (rather than semi-annual) filing, but the thresholds are not otherwise lowered with the intention of covering more persons as "lobbyists." (Assuming a pro rata expenditure of time and money, more persons will not necessarily qualify as "lobbyists" under the amended law, but the new provisions do have the effect of lowering by half the thresholds for minimum or sporadic lobbying efforts).

[80] 2 U.S.C. §1604(a).

[81] 2 U.S.C. §1603(a).

[82] The semi-annual reporting period runs from January 1 to June 30 and July 1 to December 31 each year. The report is due to the Clerk of the House and Secretary of the Senate 30 days later (January 30 and July 30) or on the first business day after the 30th if the 30th falls on a non-business day. (2 U.S.C. § 1604 (d)(1)).

[83] For more information on gift laws and rules, see CRS Report RS22566, *Acceptance of Gifts by Members and Employees of the House of Representatives Under New Ethics Rules of the 110th Congress*, by Jack Maskell; and CRS Report R43660, *The Receipt of Gifts by Federal Employees in the Executive Branch*, by Jack Maskell.

[84] For more information on the role of the Clerk of the House and the Secretary of the Senate in the administration of the Lobbying Disclosure Act, see CRS Report RL34377, *Lobbying Registration and Disclosure: The Role of the Clerk of the House and the Secretary of the Senate*, by Jacob R. Straus.

[85] "First Attempt at Lobbying Reform Since 1946 Fails," *CQ Almanac* (1967), at http://library.cqpress.com/cqalmanac/document.php?id=cqal67-1314712.

[86] U.S. General Accounting Office, *The Federal Regulation of Lobbying Act—Difficulties in Enforcement and Administration*, GGD-75-79, April 2, 1975, p. 7.

[87] 2 U.S.C. §1603 (a)(1).

[88] Speaker of the House of Representatives, "House Republicans Adopt Earmark Ban for the 112th Congress," press release, November 17, 2010, http://www.speaker.gov/press-release/house-republicans-adopt-earmark-ban-112thcongress. For example, see Kate Ackley, "Earmark Ban Changes Spring Season for Lobbying Firms," *Roll Call*, March 26, 2011, at http://www.rollcall.com/news/Earmark-Ban-Changes-Spring-Season-for-Lobbying-Firms-204346-1.html; and Holly Yeager, "Lack of Earmarks, Appropriations Bills Forces Lobbying Firm Van Scoyoc to Change Approach," *The Washington Post.com*, May 9, 2014, at http://www.washingtonpost.com/business/lack-of-earmarks-appropriations-bills-forces-lobbying-firm-van-scoyoc-to-change-approach/2014/05/09/9bebc310-be74-11e3-b195- dd0c1174052c_story.html.

According to House Rule XXI, clause 9, an earmark is "a provision or report language included primarily at the request of a Member, Delegate, Resident Commissioner, or Senator providing, authorizing or recommending a specific amount of discretionary budget authority, credit authority, or other spending authority for a contract, loan, loan guarantee, grant, loan authority, or other expenditure with or to an entity, or targeted to a specific State, locality or congressional district, other than through a statutory or administrative formula driven or competitive award process." Similarly, Senate Rule XLIV, paragraph 5 defines congressionally directed spending (e.g., an earmark) as "a provision or report language included primarily at the request of a Senator providing, authorizing or recommending a specific amount of discretionary budget authority, credit authority, or other spending authority for a contract, loan, loan guarantee, grant, loan authority, or other expenditure with or to an entity, or targeted to a specific State, locality or congressional district, other than through a statutory or administrative formula driven or competitive award process."

For more information on earmarks in the House, see CRS Report RS22866, *Earmark Disclosure Rules in the House: Member and Committee Requirements*, by Megan S. Lynch. For more information on earmarks in the Senate, see CRS Report RS22867, *Earmark Disclosure Rules in the Senate: Member and Committee Requirements*, by Megan S. Lynch.

[89] Timothy M. LaPira, "Lobbying in the Shadows: How Private Interests Hide from Public Scrutiny and Why That Matters," in *Interest Group Politics*, ed. Allan J. Cigler, Burdett A Loomis, and Anthony J. Nownes, 9th ed. (Washington, DC: CQ Press, 2015), p. 241.

[90] U.S. Congress, Clerk of the House of Representatives and Secretary of the Senate, "Section 6: Quarterly Reporting of Lobbying Activities," *Lobbying Disclosure Act Guidance*, December 15, 2014, at http://lobbyingdisclosure.house.gov/amendedida_guide.html#section6.

[91] For more information on the Office of Congressional Ethics, see CRS Report R40760, *House Office of Congressional Ethics: History, Authority, and Procedures*, by Jacob R. Straus.

[92] U.S. Congress, House, Office of Congressional Ethics, *Secord Quarter 2014 Report, April 2014-June 2014*," at http://oce.house.gov/disclosures/OCE_Second_Quarter_2014_Report.pdf.

[93] For example, see Megan R. Wilson, "Bombshell: Ethics Office Alleges Illegal Lobbying," *The Hill*, July 25, 2014, at http://thehill.com/business-a-lobbying/business-a-lobbying/213394-bombshell-ethics-office-alleges-illegal-lobbying.

[94] For example, see U.S. Government Accountability Office, *2012 Lobbying Disclosure: Observations on Lobbyists' Compliance with Disclosure Requirements*, GAO-13-437, April 2013, at http://www.gao.gov/assets/660/653471.pdf; and U.S. Government Accountability Office, *2013 Lobbying Disclosure: Observations on Lobbyists' Compliance with Disclosure Requirements*, GAO-14-485, May 2014, at http://www.gao.gov/assets/670/663647.pdf.

[95] For more information on enforcement of the Lobbying Disclosure Act, see CRS Legal Sidebar WSLG1056, OCE Reports First Enforcement Action Against Non-Registered Lobbyists, by Cynthia Brown; and CRS Report RL31126, *Lobbying Congress: An Overview of Legal Provisions and Congressional Ethics Rules*, by Jack Maskell.

[96] LaPira, "Lobbying in the Shadows: How Private Interests Hide from Public Scrutiny and Why That Matters," in *Interest Group Politics*, 9th ei, p. 225.

[97] 18 U.S.C. §207. For more information on the revolving door, see CRS Report R42728, *Post-Employment, "Revolving Door," Laws for Federal Personnel*, by Jack Maskell.

[98] Dan Auble, "Lobbyists 2012: Out of the Game or Under the Radar?" *Center for Responsive Politics*, March 20, 2013, at http://www.opensecrets.org/news/2013/03/lobbyists-2012-out-of-the-game-or-u/.

[99] Ibid. See also, Lee Fang, "Where Have All the Lobbyists Gone?" *The Nation*, February 19, 2014, at http://www.thenation.com/article/178460/shadow-lobbying-complex; Tim LaPira, "How Much Lobbying is There in Washington? It's DOUBLE What You Think," *Sunlight Foundation*, November 25, 2013, at http://sunlightfoundation.com/blog/2013/11/25/how-much-lobbying-is-there-in-washington-its-double-what-you-think; and Dave Wenhold, "New Administration Rules Could Trigger Lobbying Deregistration Rush," *The Hill*, September 30, 2009, at http://thehill.com/business-a-lobbying/k-street-insiders/k-street-insiders/60823-new-administration-rulescould-trigger-lobbying-deregistration-rush.

[100] LaPira, "Lobbying in the Shadows: How Private Interests Hide from Public Scrutiny and Why That Matters," in *Interest Group Politics*, 9th ed.

[101] See Association of Government Relations Professionals, "Our Mission and Strategic Plan," *About Us*, at http://grprofessionals.org/home/agrp-mission-and-strategic-plan. This organization was previously known as the American League of Lobbyists.

[102] Auble, "Lobbyists 2012: Out of the Game or Under the Radar?"

[103] LaPira, Lobbying in the Shadows: How Private Interests Hide from Public Scrutiny and Why That Matters," in *Interest Group Politics*, 9th ed., pp. 240-244.

[104] 2 U.S.C. §1603, note.

[105] Richard L. Hasen, "Lobbying, Rent-Seeking, and the Constitution," *Stanford Law Review*, vol. 64, no. 1 (January 2012), pp. 191-253.

[106] Jacob R. Straus, Wendy R. Ginsberg, Amanda K. Mullan, and Jaclyn D. Petruzzelli, "Restricting Membership: Assessing Agency Compliance and the Effects of Banning Federal Lobbyists from Executive Branch Advisory Committee Service," *Presidential Studies Quarterly*, vol. 42, no. 1 (June 2015), pp. 310-334. Beginning in September 2009 and finalized in October 2011, the Obama Administration issued guidance to discourage the

appointment of registered lobbyists to federal advisory committees. A study has found that this "ban" was generally effective in removing lobbyists from the United States Trade Representatives advisory committees and that this likely reflects an overall trend to reduce the number of lobbyists across all advisory committees. For more information on the Federal Advisory Committee Act, see CRS Report R40520, *Federal Advisory Committees: An Overview*, by Wendy Ginsberg.

[107] Jonathan C. Zellner, "Artificial Grassroots Advocacy and the Constitutionality of Legislative Identification and Control Measures," *Connecticut Law Review*, vol. 43, no 1 (November 2010), pp. 357-400; and Phil Harris and Conor McGrath, "Political Marketing and Lobbying: A Neglected Perspective and Research Agenda," *Journal of Political Marketing*, vol. 11, no. 1-2 (March 2012), pp. 75-94.

[108] Frank R. Baumgartner and Beth L. Leech, "Interest Niches and Policy Bandwagons: Patterns of Interest Group Involvement in National Politics," *The Journal of Politics*, vol. 63, no 4 (November 2001), p. 1205.

[109] Beth Lynn Leech, "Lobbying Strategies of American Interest Groups," (Ph.D. diss., Texas A&M University, 1998).

[110] Daniel E. Bergan, "Does Grassroots Lobbying Work?: A Field Experiment Measuring the Effects of an e-Mail Lobbying Campaign on Legislative Behavior," *American Politics Research* vol. 37, no. 2 (March 2009), p. 329.

[111] For more information on legal issues surrounding the possible regulation of grassroots lobbying, see CRS Report RL33794, *Grassroots Lobbying: Constitutionality of Disclosure Requirements*, by Jack Maskell.

[112] S. 1 (110th Congress), introduced January 4, 2007. Enacted as P.L. 110-81, the final version of HLOGA did not include provisions regulating grassroots lobbying.

[113] S. 1, §220 (b)(2).

[114] S. 1, §220 (c).

[115] Sen. Robert Bennett, "Legislative Transparency and Accountability Act of 2007—Continued," remarks in the Senate, Congressional Record, vol. 153, part 1 (January 17, 2007), 1381.

[116] Ibid., p. 1382.

[117] Sen. Joseph Lieberman, "Legislative Transparency and Accountability Act of 2007—Continued," remarks in the Senate, *Congressional Record*, vol. 153, part 1 (January 17, 2007), 1395.

[118] "Legislative Transparency and Accountability Act of 2007—Resumed," *Congressional Record*, vol. 153, part 2 (January 18, 2007), pp. 1690-1691.

[119] Burdett A. Loomis and Anthony J. Nownes, "Advocacy in an Era of Inequality," in *Interest Group Politics*, ed. Allan J. Cigler, Burdett A. Loomis, and Anthony J. Nownes, 9th ed. (Washington: CQ Press, 2016), pp. 365-366.

[120] Ken Kollman, *Outside Lobbying: Public Opinion and Interest Group Strategies* (Princeton, NJ: Princeton University Press, 1998).

[121] Daniel E. Bergan, "Does Grassroots Lobbying Work?: A Field Experiment Measuring the Effects of an e-Mail Lobbying Campaign on Legislative Behavior," *American Politics Research*, vol. 37, no. 2 (March 2009), pp. 345-346.

[122] Edward T. Walker, *Grassroots for Hire: Public Affairs Consultants in American Democracy* (New York: Cambridge University Press, 2014).

[123] Walker, *Grassroots for Hire: Public Affairs Consultants in American Democracy*, p. 10.

[124] For example, see James Madison, Alexander Hamilton, and John Jay's use of the *Federalist Papers* to persuade the citizens of New York to ratify the Constitution. A copy of the

Federalist Papers can be found at https://www.congress.gov/resources/display/content/The+Federalist+Papers.

[125] Vidal Blanes, Miko Draca, and Christian Fons-Ronen, "Revolving Door Lobbyists," *American Economic Review*, vol. 102, no. 7 (December 2012), pp. 3731-3748.

[126] United States v. Nasser, 476 F.2d 1111, 1116 (7th Cir. 1973). For more information on revolving door restrictions, see CRS Report R42728, *Post-Employment, "Revolving Door," Laws for Federal Personnel*, by Jack Maskell.

[127] *Brown v. District of Columbia Board of Zoning*, 423 A.2d 1276, 1282 (D.C. App. 1980). For a discussion of appearances of improprieties, see *General Motors Corporation v. City of New York*, 501 F.2d 639, 648-652 (2d Cir. 1974).

[128] 5 C.F.R. §2637.101(c).

[129] This paragraph was written by Jack Maskell, legislative attorney in the Congressional Research Service's American Law Division. He can be reached at jmaskell@crs.loc.gov or 7-6372. For additional information, see CRS Report R42728, *Post-Employment, "Revolving Door," Laws for Federal Personnel*, by Jack Maskell.

[130] 18 U.S.C. §207(e)(1)(B) and 18 U.S.C. §207(e)(2)-(6).

[131] 18 U.S.C. §207(e)(1)(A).

[132] Executive Order 13490, "Ethics Commitments by Executive Branch Personnel," 74 *Federal Register* 4673-4678, January 21, 2009.

[133] Ibid.

[134] David Zaring, "Against Being Against the Revolving Door," *University of Illinois Law Review*, vol. 2013, no 2 (2013), pp. 507-550.

[135] Zaring, "Against Being Against the Revolving Door," and Wentong Zheng, "The Revolving Door," *Notre Dame Law Review*, vol. 90, no. 3 (2015), pp. 1265-1308.

[136] Laurence Tai and Daniel Carpenter, "SEC Capture by Revolving Door: Strengths and Weaknesses in the Evidence Base," *Law & Financial Markets Review*, vol. 8, no. 3 (September 2014), pp. 227-240.

[137] Blanes, Draca, and Fons-Ronen, "Revolving Door Lobbyists."

[138] John M. de Figueiredo and Brian Khelleher Richter, "Advancing the Empirical Research on Lobbying," *Annual Review of Political Science*, vol. 17 (2014), p. 167.

[139] Blanes, Draca, and Fons-Ronen, "Revolving Door Lobbyists."

[140] For example, see Seungahn Nah and Gergory D. Saxton, "Modeling the Adoption and Use of Social Media by Nonprofit Organizations," *New Media & Society*, vol. 15, no 2 (March 2013), pp. 294-313.

[141] Sharon B. Heaton and Allison R. Hayward, "Registration and Reporting Under the Lobbying Disclosure Act, as Amended," in *Political Activity, Lobbying Laws and Gift Rules Guide*, ed. Trevor Potter, 2nd ed., vol. 1 (Little Falls, NJ: Glasser Legalworks, 1999), pp. 5-3.

[142] U.S. Congress, Clerk of the House of Representatives, "Section 4 – Lobbying Registration," *Lobbying Disclosure Act Guidance*, at http://lobbyingdisclosure.house.gov/amended_lda_guide.html#section4. The guidance document states: "Note that a registration would not be required for pro bono clients since the monetary thresholds of Section 4(a)(3)(A)(i) in the case of a lobbying firm, or of Section 4(a)(3)(A)(ii) in the case of an organization employing in-house lobbyists, would not be met."

[143] U.S. Congress, Clerk of the House of Representatives, "Section 6 – Quarterly Reporting of Lobbying Activities: Organizations Reporting Expenses Under Section 15 (Options IRC Reporting Methods)," *Lobbying Disclosure Act Guidance*, December 14, 2014, at http://lobbyingdisclosure.house.gov/amended_lda_guide.html#section6. See also, Austin C. Clemens, "All Politics is Local, but Lobbying is Federal and Local: the Validity of LDA

Data," *Business and Politics*, vol. 16, no. 2 (August 2014), pp. 267-289. For more information on 501(c) tax exempt organizations, see CRS Report 96-264, *Frequently Asked Questions About Tax-Exempt Organizations*, by Erika K. Lunder.

[144] 2 U.S.C. §1604(c).

[145] U.S. Government Accountability Office, *2014 Lobbying Disclosure: Observations on Lobbyists' Compliance with Disclosure Requirements*, GAO-15-310, March 2015, p. 26, at http://www.gao.gov/assets/670/669270.pdf.

[146] Ibid.

[147] Matthew Barnes, "I Was a Teenage Unlobbyist: An Interview with Norman Ball," Lobbyist.info, July 7, 2015, at http://lobbyblog.com/i-was-a-teenage-unlobbyist-an-interview-with-norman-ball.

[148] U.S. Government Accountability Office, *2014 Lobbying Disclosure: Observations on Lobbyists' Compliance with Disclosure Requirements*, GAO-15-310, March 2015, at http://www.gao.gov/assets/670/669270.pdf.

[149] U.S. General Accountability Office, "Chapter 12: Acquisition of Good and Services," *Principles of Federal Appropriations Law*, 3rd ed., vol. III, GAO-08-978SP, September 2008, p. 12-143.

[150] U.S. General Accounting Office, *The Congress Should Consider Exploring Opportunities to Expand and Improve the Application of User Charges by Federal Agencies*, PAD-80-25, March 28, 1980, p. 1, at http://www.gao.gov/assets/130/129150.pdf.

[151] U.S. Department of Justice, "FARA Fee Schedule," at http://www.fara.gov/farafee.html. For additional information, see 28 C.F.R. §5.5(d).

[152] Michael D. Frakes and Melissa F. Wasserman, "The Failed Promise of User Fees: Empirical Evidence from the U.S. Patent and Trademark Office," *Journal of Empirical Legal Studies*, vol. 11, no. 4 (December 2014), p. 603. Other activities for which fees are charged include the issuance of patents (issuance fee) and the renewal of patents (maintenance fee).

[153] Clayton P. Gillette and Thomas D. Hopkins, "Federal User Fees: A Legal and Economic Analysis," *Boston University Law Review*, vol. 67, no. 5 (November 1987), p. 825.

[154] C.C. Harris, B.L. Driver, C.S. Brinkley, and R.O. Mendelsohn, "Recreation User Fees. I. Pros and Cons; II. An Economic Analysis," *Journal of Forestry*, vol. 85, no. 5 (1987), pp. 25-40.

[155] 18 U.S.C. §207(e)(1)(B); and 18 U.S.C. §207(e)(1)(A). For more information on legislative branch revolving door restrictions, see CRS Report R42728, *Post-Employment, "Revolving Door," Laws for Federal Personnel*, by Jack Maskell.

[156] The Resident Commissioner from Puerto Rico is elected to a four-year term. For more information on the Resident Commissioner, see CRS In Focus IF10241, *Puerto Rico: Political Status and Background*, by R. Sam Garrett; CRS Report R40170, *Parliamentary Rights of the Delegates and Resident Commissioner from Puerto Rico*, by Christopher M. Davis; and CRS Report R42765, *Puerto Rico's Political Status and the 2012 Plebiscite: Background and Key Questions*, by R. Sam Garrett.

[157] Senate Rule XXXVII, paragraph 12(a), provides a similar requirement. Rule XXXVII prohibits Senators from negotiating for future employment until the election of a successor.

[158] Although some courts have suggested that it is not "unlawful discrimination" to place restrictions on a Member's ability to earn outside income while serving in Congress, (*Laxalt v Kimmitt*, 78-1437 and 78-1438 (D.C.Cir.)) it is not clear whether this reasoning would extend to a prohibition on a former Member's ability to earn a salary after he or she has resigned from Congress.

[159] For more information on the role of the Clerk of the House and the Secretary of the Senate to administer the lobbying registration and disclosure system see CRS Report RL34377, *Lobbying Registration and Disclosure: The Role of the Clerk of the House and the Secretary of the Senate*, by Jacob R. Straus.

[160] Executive Order 13490, "Ethics Commitments by Executive Branch Personnel," 74 *Federal Register* 4673-4678, January 21, 2009.

In: Lobbying Regulation
Editor: Willard N. Simmons

ISBN: 978-1-63484-998-2

Chapter 2

POST-EMPLOYMENT, "REVOLVING DOOR," LAWS FOR FEDERAL PERSONNEL*

Jack Maskell

SUMMARY

Federal personnel may be subject to certain conflict of interest restrictions on private employment activities even *after* they leave service for the United States government. These restrictions— applicable when one enters private employment after having left federal government service—are often referred to as "revolving door" laws. For the most part, other than the narrow restrictions specific to procurement officials or bank examiners, these laws restrict only certain *representational* types of activities for private employers, such as lobbying or advocacy directed to, and which attempt to influence, current federal officials.

Under federal conflict of interest law, at 18 U.S.C. Section 207, federal employees in the executive branch of government are restricted in performing certain post-employment "representational" activities for private parties, including (1) a lifetime ban on "switching sides," that is, representing a private party on the same "particular matter" involving identified parties on which the former executive branch employee had worked personally and substantially for the government; (2) a two-year ban on "switching sides" on a somewhat broader range of matters which

---

* This is an edited, reformatted and augmented version of a Congressional Research Service publication R42728, prepared for Members and Committees of Congress, dated January 7, 2014.

were under the employee's official responsibility; (3) a one-year restriction on assisting others on certain trade or treaty negotiations; (4) a one-year "cooling off" period for certain "senior" officials barring representational communications to and attempts to influence persons in their former departments or agencies; (5) a new two-year "cooling off" period for "very senior" officials barring representational communications to and attempts to influence certain other high-ranking officials in the entire executive branch of government; and (6) a one-year ban on certain former high-level officials performing certain representational or advisory activities for foreign governments or foreign political parties.

In the legislative branch, this law applies the one-year "cooling off" period, as well as the restrictions on representations on behalf of official foreign entities and assistance in trade negotiations, to Members of the House and to senior legislative staff. United States Senators are subject to a two-year "cooling off" period in which they may not lobby Congress after leaving the Senate.

"Procurement personnel" in federal agencies are not only limited in their post-employment representational, lobbying, or advocacy activities on behalf of private entities after leaving government service, but they are also prohibited from receiving compensation from certain private contractors for a period of time after being responsible for procurement action on certain large contracts as government officials. Procurement personnel also have additional rules on reporting "contacts" from prospective employers who are government contractors.

The provisions of an executive order issued by President Obama on January 21, 2009, impose stricter limits on certain executive branch personnel. Full time, non-career presidential and vice-presidential appointees, including non-career appointees in the Senior Executive Service, and excepted service confidential, policy-making appointees, are barred after leaving the Administration from "lobbying" any executive branch official "covered" by the Lobbying Disclosure Act (2 U.S.C. §1602(3)), or any non-career SES appointee, for the remainder of the Administration. Additionally, all appointees who are "senior" officials subject to the statutory one-year "cooling off" period on lobbying and advocacy communications to their former agencies must now abide by such "cooling off" period for *two* years.

Conflict of interest regulations and restrictions on certain private employment opportunities for a federal officer or employee do not necessarily end with the termination of the officer's or employee's federal service. This report is intended to provide a brief history and description of the provisions of federal law restricting employment opportunities and activities of federal employees after they leave the service of the executive or legislative branches of the federal government. The conflict of interest provisions applicable after one leaves government service to enter private employment are often referred to as "revolving door" laws.

BACKGROUND: LEGISLATIVE HISTORY AND INTENT OF PROVISIONS

Post-employment, "revolving door" statutes restricting certain subsequent private employment activities of former federal officers and employees were enacted as early as 1872, and again in 1944.[1] A portion of the current statutory provision, at 18 U.S.C. Section 207, was enacted in 1962 as part of a major revision and recodification of the federal bribery and conflict of interest laws.[2] That post-employment conflict of interest law was then amended and broadened by the Ethics in Government Act of 1978,[3] which added certain one-year "cooling-off" periods for high-level executive branch personnel, limiting their post-employment advocacy activities before the federal government for one year after leaving office. After President Reagan vetoed a major congressional revision of the post-employment law which had been passed by Congress in 1988,[4] Congress adopted as part of the Ethics Reform Act of 1989 most of the changes in the vetoed legislation.[5] The statute has been amended several times since 1989, including extensive technical amendments in 1990.[6] In 2007, as part of legislation dealing with lobbying laws and internal congressional rules on gifts, changes were made to the revolving door statute increasing the one-year "cooling off" period for "very senior" executive officials and for U.S. Senators to two years, and broadening the one-year "cooling off" restrictions for covered senior Senate staff.[7]

One of the initial and earliest purposes of enacting the "revolving door" laws was to protect the government against the use of proprietary information by former employees who might use that information on behalf of a private party in an adversarial type of proceeding or matter against the government, to the potential detriment of the public interest. As noted by the United States Court of Appeals in upholding the constitutionality of the "switching sides" prohibition of 18 U.S.C. Section 207(a), "the purpose of protecting the government, which can act only through agents, from the use against it by former agents of information gained in the course of their agency, is clearly a proper one."[8]

Another interest of the government in revolving door restrictions was to limit the potential influence and allure that a lucrative private arrangement, or the prospect of such an arrangement, may have on a current federal official when dealing with prospective private clients or future employers while still with the government, that is, "that the government employee not be influenced in the performance of public duties by the thought of later reaping a benefit from a private individual."[9] In a case dealing with another federal statute which relates in part to potential future private employment of a current federal official,[10] the court noted that the statutory scheme was intended to deal with the "nagging and persistent conflicting interests of the government official who has his eye cocked toward subsequent private employment."[11] Additional interests asserted in the proposed amendments to 18 U.S.C. Section 207 in the 99th and 100th Congresses were to prevent the corrupting influence on the governmental processes of both legislating and administering the law that may occur, and the appearances of such influences, when a federal official leaves his government post to "cash in" on his "inside" knowledge and personal influence with those persons remaining in the government.[12] As noted in the post-employment regulations promulgated under the statute by the Office of Government Ethics, the provisions of the law and regulation are directed at prohibiting "certain acts by former Government employees which may reasonably give the appearance of making unfair use of prior Government employment and affiliations"[13]

These purposes in adopting limitations on former employees' private employment opportunities must, however, also be balanced against the deterrent effect that overly restrictive provisions on career movement and advancement will have upon recruiting qualified and competent persons to government service.[14] Furthermore, unduly restrictive provisions on the "revolving door" (that is, movement of government personnel into the private sector, and private sector employees into the government) may tend to isolate, or at least insulate government employees from private sector concerns, considerations, and experiences of the general public to a degree not desirable for public policy reasons.

EXECUTIVE BRANCH—REPRESENTATIONAL ACTIVITIES

A criminal statute, codified at 18 U.S.C. Section 207, applies in some respects to all employees in the executive branch after they leave government service. It restricts or regulates private "representational," lobbying, and other advocacy type activities. Some parts of the statute also apply to legislative branch officials, and those are discussed in more detail later in this report in the part dealing with legislative branch restrictions.

Section 207 of title 18 provides a series of post-employment restrictions on "representational" activities for executive branch personnel when they leave government service, including (1) a lifetime ban on "switching sides" on a matter involving specific parties on which any executive branch employee had worked personally and substantially while with the government; (2) a two-year ban on "switching sides" on a somewhat broader range of matters which were under the employee's official responsibility; (3) a one-year restriction on assisting others on certain trade or treaty negotiations; (4) a one-year "cooling off" period for certain "senior" officials barring representational communications before their former departments or agencies; (5) a two-year "cooling" period for "very senior" officials barring representational communications to and attempts to influence certain other high ranking officials in the entire executive branch of government; and (6) a one-year ban on certain officials in performing some representational or advisory activities for foreign governments or foreign political parties.[15] Additionally, certain presidential and vice-presidential appointees in the Obama Administration are required to sign an ethics agreement which will further limit their post-government-employment lobbying and advocacy activities during the entire tenure of the Obama Administration and, for certain "senior" appointees, for one more year after leaving government service.

1. Lifetime Ban on "Switching Sides"

Section 207(a)(1) of title 18 of the United States Code provides a lifetime ban on every employee of the executive branch of the federal government "switching sides," that is, representing a private party before or against the United States government in relation to a "particular matter" involving "specific parties," when that employee had worked on that *same* matter involving those parties "personally and substantially" for the government while in its employ. This lifetime ban is a fairly narrow and case-specific restriction which in practice would apply to one who, after working substantially on a particular governmental matter such as a specific contract, a particular investigation, or a certain legal action involving specifically identified private parties, then leaves the government and attempts to represent those private parties before the government on that same, specific matter. The "switching sides" prohibition does not generally apply to broad policy making matters, including rulemaking of an agency, but rather, as noted by the Office of Government Ethics, "typically involves a specific proceeding affecting the legal rights of the parties or an isolatable transaction or related set of transactions between identifiable parties."[16]

This provision does *not* prohibit a former government official from doing *all* work for a private company or firm merely because the firm had done business with or had been regulated by the official's agency, or even had been directly affected by the former official's duties or responsibilities on a particular matter such as a contract. Rather, this particular prohibition is upon subsequent representational or professional advocacy types of activities, that is, where the former official makes "any communication or ... appearance" to or before the government "with the intent to influence" the government on the same matter on which the former official had personally and substantially worked while with the government.[17]

2. Two-Year Ban on "Switching Sides"

Section 207(a)(2) provides a two-year ban on all federal employees in the executive branch on the same types of representational, post-employment conduct involved in the lifetime ban, except that it extends to matters which were merely under the "official responsibility" of the federal official while he or she was with the government. This two-year restriction, while more limited in time than the previous ban discussed, is potentially broader in matters covered, as it does not require that the former government employee had personal and substantial involvement in the matter when that individual worked for the government, but rather merely that it was under his or her official responsibility.

3. Representations in Treaty or Trade Negotiations

Section 207(b)(1) of title 18 applies to all officers and employees of the executive branch (as well as Members of Congress and employees in the legislative branch) who had personally and substantially participated in ongoing trade or treaty negotiations on behalf of the United States within the last year of their employment and had access to certain non-public information. The law prohibits such former federal officers or employees, for one year after leaving the government, from representing, aiding, or advising anyone, on the basis of such information, concerning United States trade or treaty negotiations.

4. "Senior" Officials: One-Year "Cooling Off" Period

Section 207(c)(1) provides a one-year "no contact" or "cooling off" period for "senior" level employees in the executive branch, whereby such former employees may not make advocacy contacts or representations to (that is, communications with "intent to influence"), or any appearance before officers or employees of their former departments or agencies, for one year after such senior level employees leave those departments or agencies. "Senior" level officers or employees of the executive branch include persons paid on the Executive Schedule, and those who are paid at a rate under other authority which is equal to or greater than 86.5% of the basic rate of pay for level II of the Executive Schedule; military officers in a pay grade of 0-7 or above; and certain staff of the President and Vice President. This one-year ban applies to *any* matter on which one seeks official action by the employee's former department or agency, regardless of whether or not the former official had worked on the matter while with the government. As discussed in more detail below, "senior" executive officials who are also covered full-time presidential or vice-presidential "appointees" in the Obama Administration will be covered by this restriction, under required ethics agreements, for an additional one year. Since this "cooling off" ban applies to communications to one's former agency or department in the executive branch, it does not restrict former executive branch officials from leaving the government and then immediately "lobbying" the United States Congress, its Members, or its employees.

5. "Very Senior" Officials: Two-Year "Cooling Off" Period

The restrictions of 18 U.S.C. Section 207(d) apply to "very senior" officials of the executive branch, including the Vice President, officials compensated at level I of the Executive Schedule (Cabinet officers and certain other high-ranking officials), and employees of the Executive Office of the President and certain White House employees compensated at level II of the Executive Schedule. These officials, under amendments made to the law in 2007, may not for two years after leaving the government make representations or advocacy contacts on *any* matter before their former agencies, or to any person in an executive level position I through V in *any* department or agency of the entire executive branch of the federal government.[18] Similar to the cooling off period for "senior" level employees, these restrictions on "very senior" officials do *not* prohibit any former executive branch official from leaving the federal government and immediately lobbying Congress.

6. Representing Foreign Governments

18 U.S.C. Section 207(f) bars, for one year after leaving the government, all "senior" or "very senior" employees of the executive branch (as well as Members of Congress and senior legislative staff)[19] from performing certain duties in the area of representational or advocacy activities for or on behalf of a foreign government or a foreign political party, before any agency, department, or official in the entire U.S. government. This provision prohibits, for one year after leaving the government, those covered former officials from representing an official foreign entity "before any officer or employee of any department or agency of the United States" with intent to influence such United States official in his or her official duties,[20] and prohibits for one year, as well, a former senior or very senior official (including Members of Congress and senior legislative staff) from even *aiding* or *advising* a foreign entity "with the intent to influence a decision of any officer or employee of any department or agency of the United States."[21] The definitions within this law expressly indicate that those officers and employees *to* whom such communications on behalf of foreign governments may not be made during this one-year period include Members of Congress.[22] This one-year ban on representing or aiding or assisting in representations of foreign governments becomes a lifetime ban in the case of the United States Trade Representative or the Deputy United States Trade Representative.

The Office of Government Ethics has explained that the prohibition involves employment activities with a foreign government that bear upon attempts to influence an official of the U.S. government. Employment generally with a foreign government is not prohibited by this law, and general public relations or commercial activities for or on behalf of a foreign government might not involve the types of conduct prohibited unless they also involved attempts to influence United States government officials:

A former senior or very senior employee "represents" a foreign entity when he acts as an agent or attorney for or otherwise communicates or makes an appearance on behalf of that entity to or before any employee of a department or agency. He "aids or advises" a foreign entity when he assists the entity other than by making such a communication or appearance. Such "behind the scenes" assistance to a foreign entity could, for example, include drafting a proposed communication to an agency, advising on an appearance before a department, or consulting on other strategies designed to persuade departmental or agency decisionmakers to take certain action. A former senior or very senior employee's representation, aid, or advice is only prohibited if made or rendered with the intent to influence an official discretionary decision of a current departmental or agency employee.[23]

7. Presidential and Vice-Presidential "Appointees" in Obama Administration

President Obama issued an executive order on January 21, 2009, which places two additional post-employment, "revolving door" restrictions on all full-time, non-career presidential or vice presidential appointees in the executive branch, including non-career SES appointees and appointees to positions in the excepted service which are of a confidential and policy-making nature (such as Schedule C appointees). These "appointees" must agree to a binding "ethics pledge" which will prohibit them, after leaving government service, from lobbying (that is, acting as a registered lobbyist under the Lobbying Disclosure Act of 1995, as amended [hereinafter LDA]) any executive branch official "covered" under the LDA (2 U.S.C. §1602(3)), or any non-career SES appointee, for the remainder of the entire Obama Administration.[24]

Additionally, all such "appointees" who are also "senior" executive branch officials covered by the one-year "cooling off" period of 18 U.S.C. Section 207(c)(1), whereby such former officials may not lobby or make advocacy communications to certain officials in their former agencies and departments, must now abide by such "cooling off" period for *two* years.[25]

BANK EXAMINERS

Under amendments to the Federal Deposit Insurance Act, certain officers and employees of a "Federal banking agency or a Federal reserve bank," who are involved in bank examinations or inspections, are restricted from *any* compensated employment with those private depository institutions for a period of one year after leaving federal service.[26] This restriction applies to employees who served for at least two months during their last year of federal service as "the senior examiner (or a functionally equivalent position)," and who exercised "continuing, broad responsibility for the examination (or inspection)" of a depository institution or depository institution holding company. These former employees are barred for one year from receiving any compensation as an "employee, officer, director, or consultant" from the depository institution, the depository institution holding company that controls such depository institution, or any other company that controls the depository institution, or from the depository institution holding company or any depository institution that is controlled by that the depository institution holding company.

PROCUREMENT OFFICIALS

Further limitations upon the post-government employment activities of certain officials exist under so-called "procurement integrity" provisions of federal law for those former federal officials who had acted as contracting officers or who had other specified contracting or procurement functions for an agency. These additional restrictions go beyond the prohibitions on merely "representational," lobbying, or advocacy activities on behalf of private entities before the government, and extend also to any compensated activity for or on behalf of certain private contractors for a period of time after a former procurement official had worked on certain contracts for the government.

The current post-employment restrictions within the procurement integrity provisions of federal law are codified at 41 U.S.C. Sections 2103 and 2104. Under such provisions, former federal officials who were involved in certain contracting and procurement duties for the government concerning contracts in excess of $10 million may generally not receive any compensation from the private contractor involved, as an employee, officer, consultant, or director of that contractor, for one year after performing those procurement duties for the government.[27]

The types of contracting duties and decisions for the government which would trigger coverage under these provisions include acting as the "procuring contracting officer, the source selection authority, a member of the source selection evaluation board, or the chief of a financial or technical evaluation team in a procurement" in excess of $10 million; serving as the program manager, deputy program manager, or administrative contracting officer for covered contracts; or being an officer who personally made decisions awarding a contract, subcontract, modification of a contract, or task order or delivery order in excess of $10 million, establishing overhead or other rates valued in excess of $10 million, or approving payments or settlement of claims for a contract in excess of the covered amount.

Officials of the Department of Defense who are involved personally and substantially in procurements of over $10 million, are leaving the department, and know that they will be receiving compensation from a defense contractor within the next two years must request, within 30 days before their departure, an ethics opinion about what they can and cannot do for the defense contractor under current ethics laws and rules.[28]

NEGOTIATING PRIVATE EMPLOYMENT

Under legislation adopted in 2012, all "senior" officers and employees in the federal government will now have to report to their ethics offices negotiations that they are having for subsequent private employment. The "STOCK Act," enacted in April of 2012,[29] requires all of those federal officials who are required to file public financial disclosure reports (that is, generally, those earning a rate of salary equal to or more than 120% of the base salary for a GS-15)[30] to notify their ethics office in writing within three business days of the commencement of such "negotiations," and then to recuse themselves from any governmental matter for which such negotiations may create a conflict of interest.[31]

Executive Branch

In addition to the general reporting of negotiations under the STOCK Act by certain high-level officials, all federal employees in the executive branch who are seeking private employment may also incur restrictions on the performance of their current duties for the government under other provisions of federal law. The principal federal conflict of interest law, which is a criminal provision at 18 U.S.C. Section 208, states, among other restrictions, that once any federal employee or officer in the executive branch begins "negotiating" subsequent employment with a private employer, that employee must disqualify (recuse) himself or herself from any official governmental duties, such as recommendations, advice, or decision making, on any particular matter which has a direct and predictable effect on the financial interests of that potential private employer.[32]

The Office of Government Ethics has issued regulations concerning this potential conflict of interest, and has expanded by regulation certain disqualification requirements beyond bilateral "negotiations," applying such requirements where the employee has even merely "begun seeking employment." The regulations note that a federal employee has "begun seeking employment" not only if the employee is involved in a "discussion or communication" that is "mutually conducted" (even if the specifics of a job or employment are not discussed), but also if the employee has made an unsolicited communication regarding employment (other than merely asking for an application or sending a resume to someone who is affected by the employee's duties "only as part of an industry or other discrete class"), or if the employee has made a response other than a rejection to an unsolicited communication from a private source concerning employment. This status of "seeking employment" will continue until all possibilities of employment are rejected, and discussion ended, or two months have passed after an unsolicited communication had been made by the employee and no indication or interest or postponement of consideration was indicated.[33] During the time one is within this status of "seeking employment," the employee "should notify the person responsible for his assignment," or if the individual is responsible for his or her own assignments, then the employee must take "whatever steps are necessary" to ensure compliance. Appropriate oral or written communication to one's coworkers and supervisors concerning a required disqualification is suggested in the regulations, although written documentation of a recusal is not required in the regulations except to conform to a previous ethics agreement with the Office of Government Ethics.[34] Waivers from the disqualification requirements may be obtained in writing from the official responsible for the employee's appointment.[35]

In the area of procurement, even if no actual negotiations with a potential private employer are involved or have begun, certain "contacts" about prospective private employment between certain private contractors and federal procurement personnel may trigger reporting and recusal requirements. Agency officials who are "participating personally and substantially" in a federal procurement for a contract in excess of $100,000 must report all contacts from or to a bidder or offeror on that contract, when those contacts are about the possibility for non-federal employment for that official.[36] This includes even "unsolicited communications from offerors regarding possible employment.... "[37] In addition to reporting the contacts made or received, the official must then either reject the possibility of future employment, or must disqualify himself or herself from further participation in the procurement until all discussions have ended without an employment agreement, or until the business is no longer a bidder or offeror in that procurement.[38] Reports from procurement personnel on contacts and recusals are retained by the agency for two years, and "shall be made available to the public upon request."[39] As noted in the previous section, procurement officials in the Department of Defense who are involved personally and substantially in procurements of over $10 million, are leaving the department, and know that they will be receiving compensation from a defense contractor within the next two years must request, within 30 days before their departure, an ethics opinion about what they can and can not do for the defense contractor under current ethics laws and rules.[40]

Legislative Branch

Changes in the rules of the House and Senate were adopted in 2007 regarding negotiations for future private employment by Members and certain staff. In the Senate, the general rule is that Senators may not begin private employment negotiations, or have arrangements for subsequent private employment, until their successors have been elected.[41] In the House, the general rule is that Members may not begin private employment negotiations, or have arrangements for subsequent private employment, while still serving in the House.[42] The exception to both the House and Senate rules allows for such negotiations to begin earlier, before a successor is elected in the Senate or one's term is over in the House, if the Senator or Representative makes a disclosure statement within three business days concerning the commencement of such negotiations or agreements. However, in the Senate, this exception will not apply to, and thus will not allow, such negotiations or arrangements for future private employment which involves "lobbying activities" until the Senator's successor has been elected.[43]

The congressional rules further provide that a Member of the House of Representative who is negotiating or has an arrangement for future employment prior to the expiration of his or her term of office must "recuse" or disqualify himself or herself from participating in any matter that may raise a conflict of interest, or the appearance of a conflict of interest, because of such negotiations or employment arrangements, and must notify the House Committee on Standards of Official Conduct of such recusal.[44] In the Senate, the original disclosure statement of negotiations or arrangements is to be made public at the time it is made to the Secretary of the Senate; while in the House, the original notification of private employment negotiations or arrangements is not made public until and unless the Member must recuse himself or herself for conflict of interest purposes, and then the recusal notification as well as the original disclosure statement are made public.[45]

"Senior" staff in both the House and Senate (i.e., those employees who are compensated in excess of 75% of a Member's salary) must notify the appropriate ethics committee within three business days that the staffer is negotiating or has any agreement concerning future private employment.[46] Covered Senate and House employees must then recuse themselves from official legislative matters that raise conflicts of interest because of their prospective private employment interests, and notify the appropriate ethics committees of such recusal. Covered Senate staffers must specifically recuse themselves from making any contact or communications with the prospective employer on issues of legislative interest to that employer.

The new provisions enacted under the STOCK Act in April of 2012 may affect staff who are not necessarily covered by the House or Senate Rule provisions, since the salary threshold is lower under the statutory provisions. As noted above, any staff person who is required to file public financial disclosure reports[47] is required to notify his or her ethics office in writing within three business days of the commencement of any private employment "negotiations," and then to recuse himself or herself from any governmental matter for which such negotiations may create a conflict of interest.[48]

LEGISLATIVE BRANCH—
REPRESENTATIONAL ACTIVITIES

The Ethics Reform Act of 1989 added post-employment restrictions for Members and certain senior congressional staffers, effective January 1, 1991, and these were amended by the lobbying and ethics reform legislation, titled the "Honest Leadership and Open Government Act of 2007."[49] Under the criminal provisions of this statute, individuals who were Members of the House are prohibited from "lobbying" or making advocacy communications on behalf of any other person to current Members of either house of Congress, or to any legislative branch employee, for one year after the individual leaves Congress. For a period of two years after leaving the Senate, Senators are prohibited from similar post-employment advocacy. Additionally, senior staff employees are subject to certain one-year "cooling off" periods regarding their advocacy contacts with their former offices; and both former Members and former senior staff are limited in representing official foreign interests before the U.S. government, and in taking part in certain trade and treaty negotiations, for one year after leaving congressional service.

1. "Cooling Off" Periods on Lobbying or Advocacy

There are now so-called "cooling off" periods of two different durations applicable in the legislative branch that restrict post-employment "lobbying" and advocacy activities. United States Senators are subject to a *two-year* post-employment advocacy ban, which restricts their lobbying anyone in Congress, or any employee of a legislative office, for two years after leaving the Senate.[50] Members of the House of Representatives, as well as "senior" legislative branch employees, are now subject to a one-year "cooling off" or "no contact" period after they leave congressional office or employment.[51] Members of the House of Representatives are prohibited for one year after leaving office from lobbying or making other advocacy contacts with any Member, officer, or employee of either house of Congress, or to any employee of a legislative office.[52]

"Senior" legislative branch employees are subject to the post-employment restrictions if they are compensated at a rate equal to or above 75% of the rate of pay of a Member of the House or Senate, and are employed for more than 60 days.[53] "Senior" *Senate* staff covered by these statutory provisions are prohibited for one year after leaving Senate employment from making advocacy communications to any officer, employee, or Member of the entire Senate.[54] "Senior" *House* staff are barred for one year after leaving House employment from making advocacy communications only to their former employing office; that is, former "senior" employees of a Member of the House may not, for one year after they leave congressional employment, make advocacy or representational contacts to that Member or any of the Member's employees. House committee staffers covered by these provisions are barred for one year after leaving office from making such advocacy contacts and representations to any Member or employee of their former committees, or to any Member who was on the committee during the last year of the staffer's employment; and "senior" employees in House leadership offices are prohibited for one year after leaving employment from making advocacy communications to anyone in that leadership office.[55]

Not all contacts or communications by former Members or employees with current Members or employees within the one-year period are barred, however. The prohibition goes only to advocacy-type communications, that is, communications "with the intent to influence" a Member or officer or employee of the legislative branch concerning "any matter on which such person seeks official action" by that Member, officer, or employee, or by either house of Congress. There are also several specific exceptions to the general prohibition, including, for example, exceptions for lobbying and advocacy work for state or local governments, testifying on matters under oath, and generally for representations or communications on behalf of political candidates, parties, and political organizations.[56]

2. Trade or Treaty Negotiations

All officers and employees of the government, including Members of Congress and congressional staff, who worked personally and substantially on a treaty or trade negotiation and who had access to information not subject to disclosure under the Freedom of Information Act, may not use such information for one year after leaving the government for the purpose of aiding, assisting, advising, or representing anyone other than the United States regarding such treaty or trade negotiation.[57]

3. Representing Foreign Governments

Members of Congress, and those "senior" legislative branch employees who are covered by the one-year "cooling off" periods, are also prohibited for a year after leaving office or employment from representing an official foreign entity before the United States, or aiding or advising such entity with intent to influence any decision of an agency or employee of any agency or department of the U.S. government.[58]

4. Lobbying Restrictions on Senate Staff

All employees of the Senate remain subject to the Senate Rule governing lobbying after they leave Senate employment. Senate Rule XXXVII, clause 9, applies to all former staffers who have become registered lobbyists, or are employed by a registered lobbyist or by an entity that retains lobbyists if the former staffer is to influence legislation. Such former staffers are prohibited for one year after leaving the Senate from lobbying the Senator for whom they used to work or the Senator's staff. Former committee staff are prohibited from lobbying the Members or the staff of that committee for one year. If the staffer is a "senior" employee, then the former staffer, in accordance with the statutory restriction, will be barred from lobbying any Member, officer, or employee of the entire Senate for one year.[59]

5. Floor Privileges of Former Members

Under congressional rules and practice, former Members are generally granted the privilege of admission to the floor of the Senate or House, respectively.[60] However, under the Rules of the House of Representatives, former Members of the House are not to be entitled to floor privileges if they have any "direct or pecuniary interest in any legislative measure pending before the House or reported by any committee," and are not entitled to admission if they are registered lobbyists or agents of a foreign principal, or employed by or otherwise represent "any party or organization for the purpose of influencing, directly or indirectly, the passage, defeat or amendment of any legislative measure pending before the House, reported by any committee" or under consideration of a committee.[61] The Senate rules have also been changed to withdraw floor privileges from a former Member or officer who is a registered lobbyist or agent of a foreign principal, or is in the employ of an organization for the purpose of influencing, directly or indirectly, the passage or defeat of legislation or any legislative proposal.[62] The House and Senate have both limited the access of such former Members, if those former Members are registered lobbyists or foreign agents, to the athletic and exercise facilities in the House and Senate.[63]

6. Acceptance of Civil Office by Retiring Member of Congress

A Member of Congress may not, before the expiration of his or her term, accept a civil office in the U.S. government if that office was created, or the salary for the office had been increased during the Member's current term.[64] This constitutional provision would by its terms prevent a Member of Congress from retiring from Congress before his or her current term has expired, and accepting such a civil position with the federal government. It may be noted that the disqualification has on many occasions been avoided in regard to an office for which the salary was increased during the Member's term, by enacting legislation lowering the salary of that particular office back to its previous level.[65]

End Notes

[1] 17 Stat. 202 (1872); 58 Stat. 668 (1944) and 41 Stat. 131 (1919), recodified at 18 U.S.C. §284, June 25, 1948, 62 Stat. 698. See discussion in The Association of the Bar of the City of New York, Special Committee on Conflict of Interest Laws, CONFLICT OF INTEREST AND FEDERAL SERVICE, at 44-53 (1960).

[2] P.L. 87-849, 76 Stat. 119, October 23, 1962; see H.Rept. 748, 87th Cong., 1st Sess. (1961).

[3] P.L. 95-521, Title V, 92 Stat. 1824, 1864, October 26, 1978.

[4] S. 2334, 99th Congress (Senator Thurmond), was reported out favorably by the Senate Judiciary Committee (S.Rept. No. 99-396, 99th Cong., 2d Sess. (1986)), and in the 100th Congress the Senate Judiciary Committee again reported out legislation amending the post-employment laws (S. 237, S.Rept. No. 100-101, 100th Cong., 1st Sess. (1987)). An amendment in the nature of a substitute was offered by Senator Thurmond for himself and Senators Metzenbaum, Levin, and Specter on February 3, 1988, and the legislation (S. 237) was amended on the Senate floor and passed on April 19, 1988. In the House, the Judiciary Committee reported out a clean bill (H.R. 5043) on October 6, 1988 (H.R. Rpt. No. 100-1068, 100th Cong., 2d Sess.), which passed the House on October 12, 1988. Amendments were offered to the House bill and agreed to in the Senate on October 18, and after the House substituted compromise provisions for the bill, the House and Senate passed the legislation on October 21, 1988. The legislation was formally presented to the President on

November 14, 1988, subsequent to the adjournment of the 100th Congress. The President announced his intention not to sign the bill on November 23, 1988, and issued a statement of disapproval. The "pocket veto" was effective on November 25, 1988, upon the President's failure to sign the bill.

[5] P.L. 101-194, Title I, §101(a), 103 Stat. 1716, November 30, 1989, as amended.

[6] P.L. 101-280, 104 Stat. 149, May 4, 1990.

[7] P.L. 110-81, September 14, 2007. See, S. 1, 110th Congress, Sections 101-105, 301, 531-532.

[8] United States v. Nasser, 476 F.2d 1111, 1116 (7th Cir. 1973).

[9] Brown v. District of Columbia Board of Zoning, 423 A.2d 1276, 1282 (D.C. App. 1980); note General Motors Corporation v. City of New York, 501 F.2d 639, 648-652 (2d Cir. 1974), as to appearances of improprieties in such situations.

[10] 18 U.S.C. §208, which prohibits, in part, a federal employee from taking any official action for the government on a matter in which a firm or organization "with whom he is negotiating ... prospective employment, has a financial interest.... "

[11] United States v. Conlon, 628 F.2d 150, 155, n. 26 (D.C. Cir. 1980), quoting CONFLICT OF INTEREST AND FEDERAL SERVICE, supra at 234.

[12] See, generally, discussion in S.Rept. No. 396, 99th Cong., 2d Sess. (1986), and S.Rept. No. 101, 100th Cong., 1st Sess. (1987).

[13] 5 C.F.R. §2637.101(c).

[14] S.Rept. No. 170, 95th Cong., 1st Sess. 32 (1978); note discussion in President's Commission on Federal Ethics Law Reform, "To Serve With Honor," Report and Recommendations to the President, at 53 (1989).

[15] An executive order, 12834, January 20, 1993, issued by President Clinton, had required senior presidential appointees to full-time government positions to take an "ethics pledge" which required observance of longer time periods, generally five-years, for some of the restrictions on private employment after leaving their government posts. That executive order was revoked on December 28, 2000 (E.O. 13184), and similar five-year bans were not re-instituted in the subsequent Bush Administration. An "ethics pledge" and further "revolving door" restrictions were instituted by the Obama Administration for certain high-level appointees (note discussion in this report on p. 6).

[16] 5 C.F.R. §2637.201(c).

[17] See Office of Government Ethics Regulations, at 5 C.F.R. §§2637.101(c)(5), 2637.201(b).

[18] 18 U.S.C. §207(d)(1) and (2), P.L. 110-81, Section 101(a).

[19] For those positions and compensation levels included in "senior" and "very senior" designations, see 18 U.S.C. §207(c)(2), (d)(1), and (e)(1)-(7).

[20] 18 U.S.C. §207(f)(1)(A).

[21] 18 U.S.C. §207(f)(1)(B).

[22] 18 U.S.C. §207(i)(1)(B).

[23] Office of Government Ethics Memorandum "Revised Material Relating to 18 U.S.C. §207," November 5, 1992, at p. 11.

[24] Executive Order 13490, Section 5 (74 F.R. 4673-4674, January 26, 2009).

[25] Executive Order 13490, Section 4.

[26] P.L. 108-458, §6303(b), 118 Stat. 3751 (2004); see now 12 U.S.C. §1820(k).

[27] 41 U.S.C. §2104(a). See exceptions to prohibtion at 41 U.S.C. §2104(b). Regulations implementing these provsions are at 48 C.F.R. §§3.104-3(d), 3.104-6.

[28] P.L. 110-181, "National Defense Authorization Act for Fiscal Year 2008," at Sec. 847, 122 Stat. 243 (2008) (10 U.S.C. §1701, note); see also regulations at 74 Federal Register 2408, January 15, 2009.

[29] P.L. 112-105, 126 Stat. 291, April 4, 2012.

[30] The reporting of negotiations applies to everyone in the federal government who is "required to file a financial disclosure report under section 101 of the Ethics in Government Act of 1978." P.L. 112-105, Section 17, 126 Stat. 303.

[31] P.L. 112-105, Section 17, 126 Stat. 303.

[32] 18 U.S.C. §208(a); note 5 C.F.R. §2635.601;United States v. Conlon, 628 F.2d 150 (D.C.Cir. 1980); CACI, Inc. - Federal v. United States, 719 F.2d 1567 (Fed. Cir. 1983).

[33] 5 C.F.R. §2635.603(b).

[34] 5 C.F.R. §2635.604(b),(c).

[35] 5 C.F.R. §2635.605; 18 U.S.C. §208(b)(1) and (3).

[36] 41 U.S.C. §2103.

[37] 48 C.F.R. §3.104-3(c)(2).

[38] 41 U.S.C.§2103(a)(2).

[39] 41 U.S.C. §2103(b).

[40] P.L. 110-181, "National Defense Authorization Act for Fiscal Year 2008," at Sec. 847, 122 Stat. 243 (2008) (10 U.S.C. §1701, note); see also regulations at 74 F.R. 2408, January 15, 2009.

[41] Senate Rule XXXVII, para. 12(a).

[42] House Rule XXVII, cl. 1 (P.L. 110-81, Sections 301 and 532), as amended by H.Res. 5, 111th Congress.

[43] Senate Rule XXXVII, para. 12(b). "Lobbying activities" referred to are those defined by the Lobbying Disclosure Act of 1995, and thus would include behind-the-scenes advice and assistance to support "lobbying contacts." See 2 U.S.C. §1602(7).

[44] House Rule XXVII, cl. 4.

[45] Senate Rule XXXVII, para. 12(a); House Rule XXVII, cl. 4.

[46] Senate Rule XXXVII, para. 12(c); House Rule XXVII, cl. 2.

[47] The reporting of negotiations applies to anyone who is "required to file a financial disclosure report under section 101 of the Ethics in Government Act of 1978" (P.L. 112-105, Section 17, 126 Stat. 303), generally those compensated at a salary rate of 120% of the base salary of a GS-15 for at least 60 days in a calendar year, or at least one principal assistant of a Member's office if no staffer is compensated above the threshold amount.

[48] P.L. 112-105, Section 17, 126 Stat. 303.

[49] P.L. 110-81, September 14, 2007.

[50] 18 U.S.C. §207(e)(1)(A).

[51] 18 U.S.C. §207(e)(1)(B) and (e)(2)-(6).

[52] 18 U.S.C. §207(e)(1)(A) and (B).

[53] 18 U.S.C. §207(e)(7).

[54] 18 U.S.C. §207(e)(1)(B), as amended by P.L. 110-81.

[55] 18 U.S.C. §207(e)(3),(4),(5), and (6).

[56] 18 U.S.C. §207(j).

[57] 18 U.S.C. §207(b)(1).

[58] 18 U.S.C. §207(f).

[59] Senate Rule XXXVII, para. 9(a) (b), and (c), as amended by P.L. 110-81 [S. 1, 110th Congress], Section 531.

[60] Senate Rule XXIII; House Rule IV, clause 2(a)(15).

[61] Rules of the House of Representatives, House Rule IV, clause 4, as amended by H.Res. 648, February 1, 2006, and regulations of the Speaker, 123 Cong. Rec. 321 (January 6, 1977).

[62] Senate Rule XXIII, P.L. 110-81, Section 533.

[63] Senate Rule XXIII, paragraph 3, P.L. 110-81, Section 533; see H.Res. 6, Section 511(c).
[64] United States Constitution, Article I, Section 6, clause 2.
[65] See general discussion in out-of-print CRS Report 87-579A, Ineligibility of a Member of Congress for a Civil Office in the Federal Government Which Was Created, or for Which the Salary Was Increased, During the Time For Which the Member Was Elected, June 30, 1987, available to congressional requesters from the author.

In: Lobbying Regulation
Editor: Willard N. Simmons
ISBN: 978-1-63484-998-2

Chapter 3

2014 LOBBYING DISCLOSURE: OBSERVATIONS ON LOBBYISTS' COMPLIANCE WITH DISCLOSURE REQUIREMENTS*

United States Government Accountability Office

WHY GAO DID THIS STUDY

LDA requires lobbyists to file quarterly lobbying disclosure reports and semiannual reports on certain political contributions. The law also requires that GAO annually audit lobbyists' compliance with the LDA. GAO's objectives were to (1) audit the extent to which lobbyists can demonstrate compliance with disclosure requirements, (2) identify challenges to compliance that lobbyists report, and (3) describe the resources and authorities available to USAO in its role in enforcing LDA compliance, and the efforts USAO has made to improve enforcement. This is GAO's eighth report under the mandate.

GAO reviewed a stratified random sample of 100 quarterly disclosure LD-2 reports filed for the third and fourth quarters of calendar year 2013 and the first and second quarters of calendar year 2014. GAO also reviewed two random samples totaling 160 LD-203 reports from year-end 2013 and midyear

* This is an edited, reformatted and augmented version of a United States Government Accountability Office publication, No. GAO-15-310, dated March 2015.

2014. This methodology allowed GAO to generalize to the population of 46,599 disclosure reports with $5,000 or more in lobbying activity, and 30,524 reports of federal political campaign contributions. GAO also met with officials from USAO to obtain status updates on its efforts to focus resources on lobbyists who fail to comply.

GAO provided a draft of this report to the Attorney General for review and comment. The Department of Justice provided a technical comment, which GAO incorporated as appropriate.

WHAT GAO FOUND

For the 2014 reporting period, most lobbyists provided documentation for key elements of their disclosure reports to demonstrate compliance with the Lobbying Disclosure Act of 1995 as amended (LDA). For lobbying disclosure (LD-2) reports and political contributions (LD-203) reports filed during the third and fourth quarter of 2013 and the first and second quarter of 2014, GAO estimates that

- 90 percent of lobbyists filed initial LD-2 reports as required for new lobbying registrations (lobbyists are required to file LD-2 reports for the quarter in which they first register).
- 93 percent could provide documentation for income and expenses. However, 21 percent of these LD-2 reports were not properly rounded to the nearest $10,000 and 6 percent of those reports listed the exact amount.
- 94 percent filed year-end 2013 reports as required.
- 14 percent of all LD-2 reports did not properly disclose one or more previously held covered positions (certain positions in the executive and legislative branches) as required.
- 4 percent of all LD-203 reports omitted one or more reportable political contributions that were documented in the Federal Election Commission database.

These findings are generally consistent with prior reports GAO issued for the 2010 through 2013 reporting periods and can be generalized to the population of disclosure reports.

Over the past several years of reporting on lobbying disclosure, GAO has found that most lobbyists in the sample rated the terms associated with LD-2 reporting as "very easy" or "somewhat easy" to understand with regard to meeting their reporting requirements. However, some disclosure reports demonstrate compliance difficulties, such as failure to disclose covered positions or misreporting of income or expenses. In addition, lobbyists amended 19 of 100 original disclosure reports in GAO's sample, changing information previously reported.

The U.S. Attorney's Office for the District of Columbia (USAO) stated it has sufficient resources and authority to enforce LD-2 and LD-203 compliance with LDA. It has one contract paralegal working full time and six attorneys working part time on LDA enforcement issues.

USAO continued its efforts to follow up on referrals for noncompliance with lobbying disclosure requirements by contacting lobbyists by e-mail, telephone, and letter. Also, USAO has finalized a settlement with a lobbyist to resolve multiple instances of noncompliance and is in the process of finalizing another settlement.

ABBREVIATIONS

Clerk of the House	Clerk of the House of Representatives
FEC	Federal Election Commission
HLOGA	Honest Leadership and Open Government Act of 2007
LDA	Lobbying Disclosure Act of 1995
SAUSA	Special Assistant United States Attorneys
USAO	U.S. Attorney's Office for the District of Columbia

* * *

March 26, 2015

Congressional Committees

The Honest Leadership and Open Government Act of 2007 (HLOGA) amended the Lobbying Disclosure Act of 1995 to require lobbyists to file quarterly lobbying disclosure reports and semiannual reports on certain political contributions.[1] HLGOA also increased civil penalties and added criminal penalties for failure to comply with lobbying disclosure requirements. In addition, HLOGA requires us to annually audit the extent of lobbyists' compliance with the Lobbying Disclosure Act of 1995 as amended (LDA) by reviewing publicly available lobbying registrations and other matters.[2] This is our eighth report under this mandate.

Our objectives were to (1) determine the extent to which lobbyists can demonstrate compliance with the requirements for registrations and reports filed under the LDA; (2) identify any challenges and potential improvements to compliance by lobbyists, lobbying firms, and registrants; and (3) describe the resources and authorities available to the U.S. Attorney's Office for the District of Columbia (USAO) in its role in enforcing LDA compliance and the efforts it has made to improve that enforcement.

To determine the extent to which lobbyists can demonstrate compliance, we examined a stratified random sample of 100 quarterly lobbying disclosure (LD-2) reports with income and expenses of $5,000 or more filed during the third and fourth quarters of calendar year 2013 and the first and second quarters of calendar year 2014. We selected the randomly sampled reports from the publicly downloadable database maintained by the Clerk of the House of Representatives (Clerk of the House).[3] A complete description of our methodology can be found in appendix I. This methodology allows us to generalize some elements to the population of LD-2 reports. We then contacted each lobbyist or lobbying firm[4] in our sample. We asked them to provide written documentation for key elements of their LD-2 reports, including the amount of income reported for lobbying activities, the amount of expenses reported, the houses of Congress or federal agencies lobbied, lobbying issue areas, and the names of lobbyists listed in the report. We also reviewed whether lobbyists listed on the LD-2 reports properly disclosed prior covered official positions, and whether the lobbyists filed the semiannual report of federal political contributions. All lobbyists in our sample responded to our requests to meet with us to review documentation. Appendix II contains a list of lobbyists and clients whose LD-2 reports we randomly selected for our review.

To determine whether lobbyists reported their federal political contributions as required by the LDA, we analyzed stratified random samples of year-end 2013 and mid-year 2014 semiannual political contributions (LD-203) reports. The samples contain 80 LD-203 reports that have contributions listed and 80 LD-203 reports that list no contributions. We selected the randomly sampled reports from the publicly downloadable contributions database maintained by the Clerk of the House. (See appendix III for a list of lobbyists and lobbying firms randomly selected for our review of LD-203 reports.) We then checked the contributions reported in the Federal Election Commission's (FEC) database against the contributions identified in our sample to determine whether all contributions reported in the FEC database were also reported on the LD-203s as required. We contacted lobbyists and asked them to provide documentation to clarify differences we observed. All lobbyists contacted complied with our request to provide documentation. This methodology allows us to generalize to the population of LD-203 reports both with and without contributions.

To determine whether lobbyists were meeting the requirement to file an LD-2 report for the quarter in which they registered, we compared new registrations (LD-1) filed in the third and fourth quarters of 2013, and the first and second quarters of 2014 to the corresponding LD-2 reports on file with the Clerk of the House.

To assess the reliability of the data used, we reviewed available documentation and interviewed knowledgeable officials. We found the data to be sufficiently reliable for our purposes. The details of the data reliability assessments are available in appendix I.

To identify challenges and potential improvements to compliance, we used a structured web-based survey to obtain views from lobbyists included in our sample of reports.

To describe the resources and authorities available to USAO and their efforts to improve LDA enforcement, we interviewed USAO officials and obtained information about their system's capabilities to track enforcement and compliance trends and referral data that it receives from the Secretary of the Senate and Clerk of the House.

The mandate does not require us to identify lobbyist organizations that failed to register and report in accordance with LDA requirements. The mandate also does not require us to determine whether reported lobbying activity or political contributions represented the full extent of lobbying activities that took place.

We conducted this performance audit from June 2014 to March 2015 in accordance with generally accepted government auditing standards. Those standards require that we plan and perform the audit to obtain sufficient, appropriate evidence to provide a reasonable basis for our findings and conclusions based on our audit objectives. We believe that the evidence obtained provides a reasonable basis for our findings and conclusions based on our audit objectives.

BACKGROUND

The LDA requires lobbyists to register with the Secretary of the Senate and the Clerk of the House and to file quarterly reports disclosing their lobbying activity. Lobbyists are required to file their registrations and reports electronically with the Secretary of the Senate and the Clerk of the House through a single entry point. Registrations and reports must be publicly available in downloadable, searchable databases from the Secretary of the Senate and the Clerk of the House. No specific statutory requirements exist for lobbyists to generate or maintain documentation in support of the information disclosed in the reports they file. However, guidance issued by the Secretary of the Senate and the Clerk of the House recommends that lobbyists retain copies of their filings and documentation supporting reported income and expenses for at least 6 years after they file their reports.

The LDA requires that the Secretary of the Senate and the Clerk of the House provide guidance and assistance on the registration and reporting requirements and develop common standards, rules, and procedures for LDA compliance. The Secretary of the Senate and the Clerk of the House review the guidance semiannually. It was last reviewed December 15, 2014. The last revision was on February 15, 2013, to (among other issues) update the reporting thresholds for inflation. The guidance provides definitions of terms in the LDA, elaborates on the registration and reporting requirements, includes specific examples of different scenarios, and provides explanations of why certain scenarios prompt or do not prompt disclosure under the LDA. The Secretary of the Senate and Clerk of the House's Offices told us they continue to consider information we report on lobbying disclosure compliance when they periodically update the guidance. In addition, they told us they e-mail registered lobbyists quarterly on common compliance issues and reminders to file reports by the due dates.

The LDA defines a lobbyist as an individual who is employed or retained by a client for compensation, who has made more than one lobbying contact (written or oral communication to a covered executive or legislative branch official made on behalf of a client), and whose lobbying activities represent at least 20 percent of the time that he or she spends on behalf of the client during the quarter.[5] Lobbying firms are persons or entities that have one or more employees who lobby on behalf of a client other than that person or entity.[6]

Lobbying firms are required to register with the Secretary of the Senate and the Clerk of the House for each client if the firms receive or expect to receive over $3,000 in income from that client for lobbying activities.[7]

Lobbyists are also required to submit a quarterly report, also known as an LD-2 report (LD-2), for each registration filed. The LD-2s contain information that includes:

- the name of the lobbyist reporting on quarterly lobbying activities and the name of the client for whom the lobbyist lobbied;
- a list of individuals who acted as lobbyists on behalf of the client during the reporting period;
- whether any lobbyists served in covered positions in the executive or legislative branch in the previous 20 years;
- codes describing general issue areas, such as agriculture and education;
- a description of the specific lobbying issues;
- houses of Congress and federal agencies lobbied during the reporting period; and
- reported income (or expenses for organizations with in-house lobbyists) related to lobbying activities during the quarter (rounded to the nearest $10,000).

The LDA also requires lobbyists to report certain political contributions semiannually in the LD-203 report. These reports must be filed 30 days after the end of a semiannual period by each lobbying firm registered to lobby and by each individual listed as a lobbyist on a firm's lobbying report. The lobbyists or lobbying firms must

- list the name of each federal candidate or officeholder, leadership political action committee, or political party committee to which they made contributions equal to or exceeding $200 in the aggregate during the semiannual period;
- report contributions made to presidential library foundations and presidential inaugural committees;
- report funds contributed to pay the cost of an event to honor or recognize a covered official, funds paid to an entity named for or controlled by a covered official, and contributions to a person or entity in recognition of an official, or to pay the costs of a meeting or other event held by or in the name of a covered official; and
- certify that they have read and are familiar with the gift and travel rules of the Senate and House and that they have not provided,

requested, or directed a gift or travel to a member, officer, or employee of Congress that would violate those rules.

The Secretary of the Senate and the Clerk of the House, along with USAO are responsible for ensuring LDA compliance. The Secretary of the Senate and the Clerk of the House notify lobbyists or lobbying firms in writing that they are not complying with the LDA reporting. Subsequently, they refer those lobbyists who fail to provide an appropriate response to USAO. USAO researches these referrals and sends additional noncompliance notices to the lobbyists or lobbying firms, requesting that they file reports or terminate their registration. If USAO does not receive a response after 60 days, it decides whether to pursue a civil or criminal case against each noncompliant lobbyist. A civil case could lead to penalties up to $200,000 for each violation, while a criminal case—usually pursued if a lobbyist's noncompliance is found to be knowing and corrupt—could lead to a maximum of 5 years in prison.

Lobbyists Filed Disclosure Reports as Required for Most New Lobbying Registrations

Generally, under the LDA, within 45 days of being employed or retained to make a lobbying contact on behalf of a client, the lobbyist must register by filing an LD-1 form with the Clerk of the House and the Secretary of the Senate. Thereafter, the lobbyist must file quarterly disclosure (LD-2) reports detailing the lobbying activities. Of the 2,950 new registrations we identified for the third and fourth quarters of 2013 and first and second quarters of 2014, we matched 2,659 of them (90 percent) to corresponding LD-2 reports filed within the same quarter as the registration. These results are consistent with the findings we have reported in prior reviews. We used the House lobbyists' disclosure database as the source of the reports and used an electronic matching algorithm that allows for misspellings and other minor inconsistencies between the registrations and reports. Figure 1 shows lobbyists filed disclosure reports as required for most new lobbying registrations from 2010 through 2014.

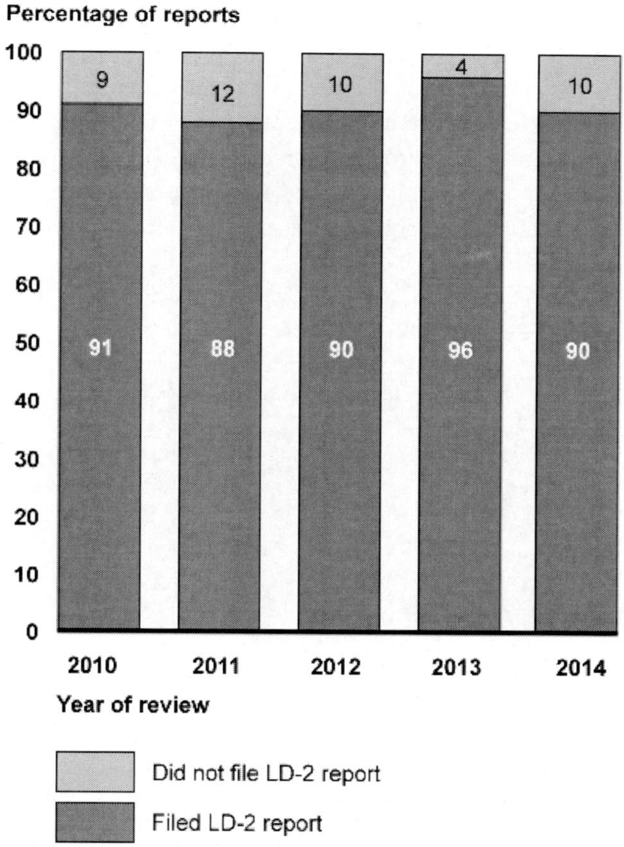

Source: GAO analysis. | GAO-15-310

Note: Results are based on an analysis of all new lobbying registrations for the periods corresponding to this review and prior GAO reviews.

Figure 1. Comparison of Newly Filed Lobbying Registrations to Initial LD-2 Reports from 2010 through 2014.

For Most LD-2 Reports, Lobbyists Provided Documentation for Key Elements but for Some LD-2 Reports, Lobbyists Rounded Their Income or Expenses Incorrectly

For selected elements of lobbyists' LD-2 reports that can be generalized to the population of lobbying reports, unless otherwise noted, our findings have been consistent from year to year. We used tests that adjusted for multiple comparisons to assess the statistical significance of changes over time.

Most lobbyists reporting $5,000 or more in income or expenses provided written documentation to varying degrees for the reporting elements in their disclosure reports. For this year's review, lobbyists for an estimated 93 percent of LD-2 reports provided written documentation for the income and expenses reported for the third and fourth quarters of 2013 and the first and second quarters of 2014. Figure 2 shows that for most LD-2 reports, lobbyists provided documentation for income and expenses for sampled reports from 2010 through 2014.

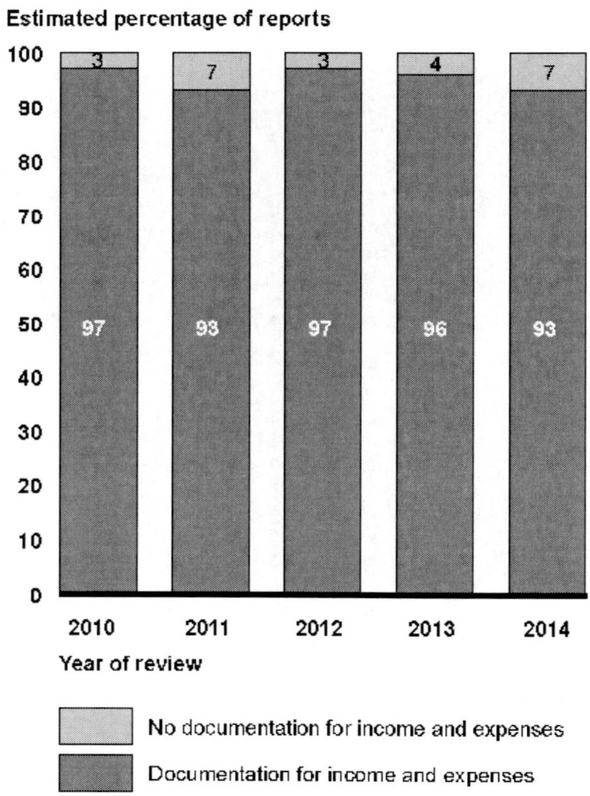

Source: GAO analysis. | GAO-15-310

Note: Estimates of proportions based on sampled reports, generalizable to the universe of LD-2 reports with lobbying activity. Results have a maximum margin of error of 12.1 percent. Year-to-year differences are not statistically significant.

Figure 2. Estimated Percentage of LD-2 Reports with Documentation for Income and Expenses from 2010 through 2014.

Figure 3 shows that for some LD-2 reports, lobbyists rounded their income or expenses incorrectly. We identified 21 percent of reports as having rounding errors. We have found that rounding difficulties have been a recurring issue for LD-2 reports from 2010 through 2014.[8] Several lobbyists who reported expenses told us that based on their reading of the LD-2 form they believed they were required to report the exact amount. While this is not consistent with the LDA or the guidance, this may be a source of some of the confusion regarding rounding errors. In 2014, 6 percent of lobbyists reported the exact amount of income or expenses.

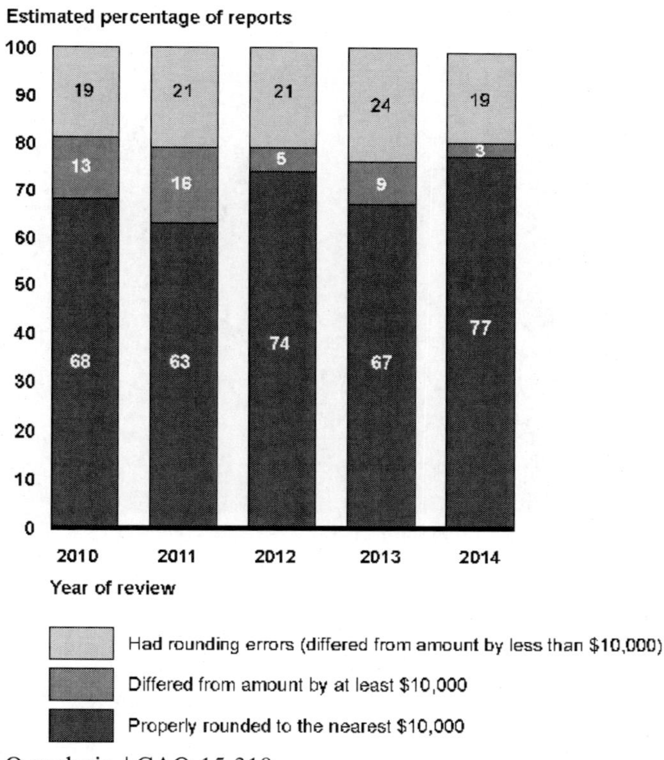

Source: GAO analysis. | GAO-15-310

Note: Estimates of proportions based on sampled reports, generalizable to the universe of LD-2 reports with lobbying activity. Estimates have a maximum margin of error of 12.1 percentage points. With the exception of the decrease in the proportion of reports with a $10,000 or greater difference from 2011 to 2012, year to year differences were not statistically significant.

Figure 3. Estimated Percentage of LD-2 Reports with Differences in Reported and Documented Amount of Income and Expenses from 2010 through 2014.

The LDA requires lobbyists to disclose lobbying contacts made to federal agencies on behalf of the client for the reporting period. This year, of the 100 LD-2 reports in our sample, 46 LD-2 reports disclosed lobbying activities at federal agencies. Of those, lobbyists provided documentation for all lobbying activities at executive branch agencies for 26 LD-2 reports.[9]

Figures 4 through 7 show that lobbyists for most LD-2 reports provided documentation for selected elements of their LD-2 reports from 2010 through 2014.

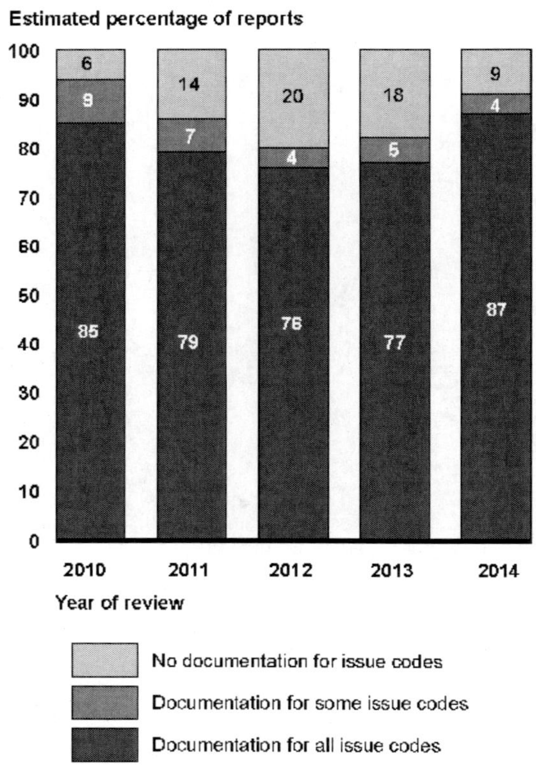

Source: GAO analysis. | GAO-15-310

Note: Estimates of proportions based on sampled reports, generalizable to the universe of LD-2 reports with lobbying activity. Estimates have a maximum margin of error of 12.1 percentage points. Year-to-year differences are not statistically significant. Issue codes are three letter codes for general lobbying topics such as education or agriculture.

Figure 4. Extent to Which Lobbyists Provided Documentation for Issue Codes from 2010 through 2014.

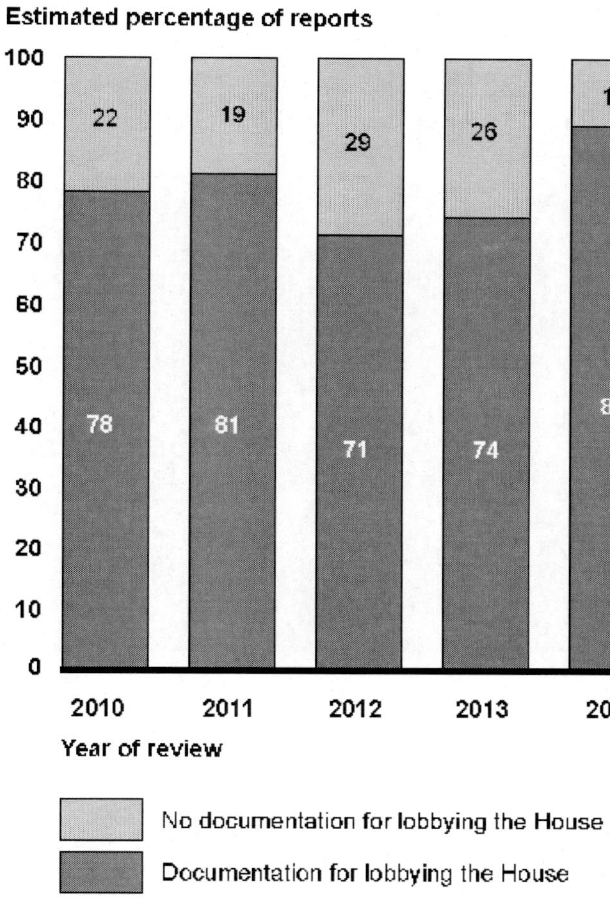

Source: GAO analysis. | GAO-15-310

Note: Estimates of proportions based on sampled reports, generalizable to the universe of LD-2 reports with lobbying activity. Estimates have a maximum margin of error of 12.1 percentage points. With the exception of the increase in the proportion of reports for which documentation was provided to support lobbying the House from 2013 to 2014, year-to-year differences are not statistically significant.

Figure 5. Extent to Which Lobbyists Provided Documentation for Lobbying the House from 2010 through 2014.

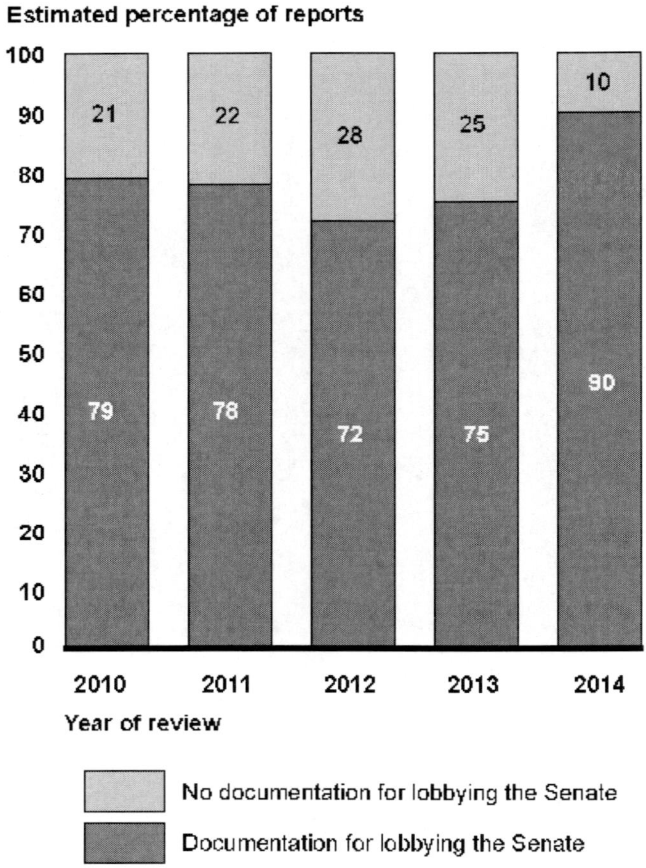

Source: GAO analysis. | GAO-15-310

Note: Estimates of proportions based on sampled reports, generalizable to the universe of LD-2 reports with lobbying activity. Estimates have a maximum margin of error of 12.1 percentage points. With the exception of the increase in the proportion of reports for which documentation was provided to support lobbying the Senate from 2013 to 2014, year-to-year differences are not statistically significant.

Figure 6. Extent to Which Lobbyists Provided Documentation for Lobbying the Senate from 2010 through 2014.

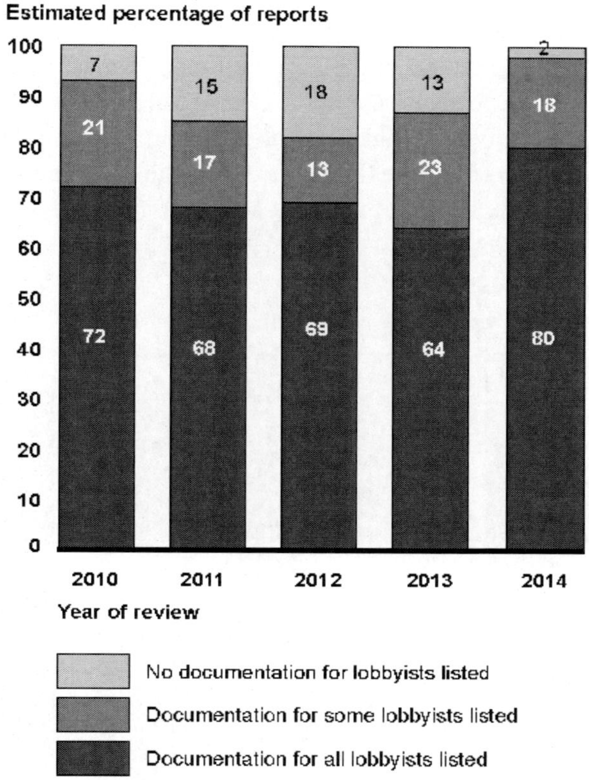

Source: GAO analysis. | GAO-15-310

Note: Estimates of proportions based on sampled reports, generalizable to the universe of LD-2 reports with lobbying activity. Estimates have a maximum margin of error of 12.1 percentage points. Year-to-year differences are not statistically significant. Documentation for individual lobbyists listed is documentation (such as emails, calendar entries, and internal memos) which supports that the lobbyist listed performed lobbying activities during the period covered by the review.

Figure 7. Extent to Which Lobbyists Provided Documentation for Individual Lobbyists Listed from 2010 through 2014.

For Most Lobbying Disclosure Reports (LD-2), Lobbyists Filed Political Contribution Reports (LD-203) for All Listed Lobbyists

Lobbyists for an estimated 94 percent of LD-2 reports filed year-end 2013 reports for all lobbyists listed on the report as required. All but two lobbying firm filed LD-203s for the lobbying firm itself before we preformed our check.

The firm that had not filed an LD-203 filed one as soon as we brought it to the firm's attention. The other firm did not respond to our request for the information about filing the LD-203. Figure 8 shows that lobbyists for most lobbying firms filed contribution reports as required in our sample from 2010 through 2014. All individual lobbyists and lobbying firms reporting lobbying activity are required to file LD-203 reports semiannually, even if they have no contributions to report, because they must certify compliance with the gift and travel rules.

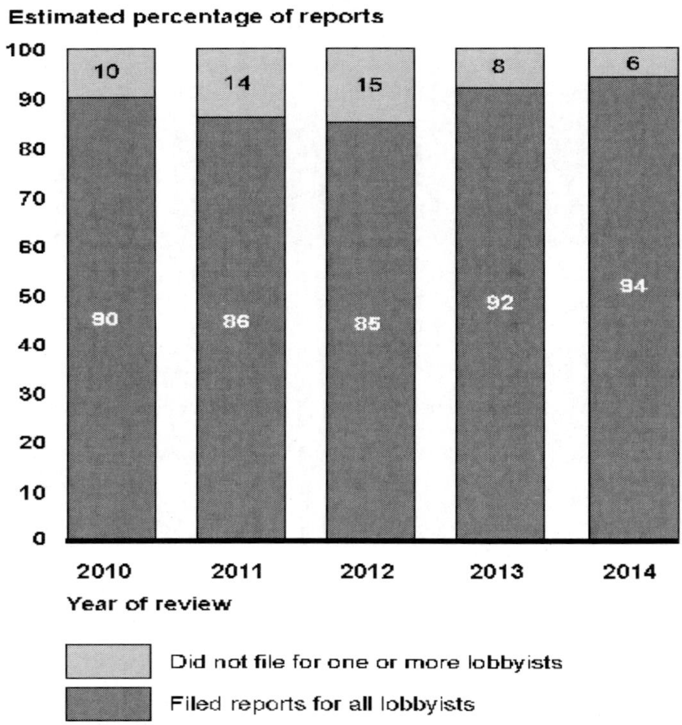

Source: GAO analysis. | GAO-15-310

Note: Estimates of proportions based on sampled reports, generalizable to the universe of LD-2 reports with lobbying activity. Estimates have a maximum margin of error of 12.1 percentage points. Year-to-year differences are not statistically significant.

Figure 8. Extent to Which Lobbyists on LD-2 Reports Filed Contribution Reports for All Listed Lobbyists from 2010 through 2014.

For Some LD-2 Reports, Lobbyists Failed to Disclose Their Previously Held Covered Positions

The LDA requires a lobbyist to disclose previously held covered positions when first registering as a lobbyist for a new client. This can be done either on the LD-1 or on the LD-2 quarterly filing when added as a new lobbyist. This year, we estimate that 14 percent of all LD-2 reports did not properly disclose one or more previously held covered positions as required. Figure 9 shows the extent to which lobbyists failed to properly disclose one or more covered positions as required from 2010 through 2014.

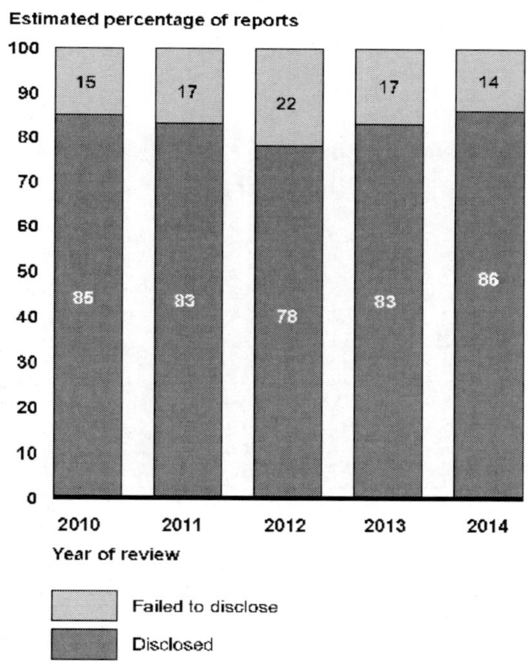

Source: GAO analysis. | GAO-15-310

Note: Estimates of proportions based on sampled reports, generalizable to the universe of LD-2 reports with lobbying activity. Estimates have a maximum margin of error of 12.1 percentage points. Year-to-year differences are not statistically significant. For this element in prior reports, we reported an estimated minimum percentage of reports based on a one-sided 95 percent confidence interval, rather than the estimated proportion as shown here.

Figure 9. Estimated Percentage of LD-2 Reports Where Lobbyists Failed to Properly Disclose One or More Covered Positions from 2010 through 2014.

Some Lobbyists Amended Their Disclosure Reports After We Contacted Them

Lobbyists amended 19 of the 100 LD- 2 disclosure reports in our original sample to make changes to previously reported information after we contacted them. Of the 19 reports, 10 were amended after we notified the lobbyists of our review, but before we met with them. An additional 9 of the 19 reports were amended after we met with the lobbyists to review their documentation. We consistently find a notable number of amended LD-2 reports in our sample each year following notification of our review. This suggests that sometimes our contact spurs lobbyists to more closely scrutinize their reports than they would have without our review.

Table 1 lists reasons lobbying firms in our sample amended their LD-1 or LD-2 reports.

Table 1. Reasons Lobbyists in GAO's Sample Amended Their Disclosure Reports

	Number of times reason selected
Update covered position	8
Change reported income or expenses	3
Change House, Senate or executive agency lobbying activity	5
Change individuals who acted as a lobbyist	4
Change general issue area code	1
Terminated their lobbying activity	1
Total	**22**

Source: GAO analysis. | GAO-15-310

Note: Some firms cited more than one reason for amending.

Most LD-203 Contribution Reports Disclosed Political Contributions Listed in the FEC Database

As part of our review, we compared contributions listed on lobbyists' and lobbying firms' LD-203 reports against those political contributions reported in the FEC database to identify whether political contributions were omitted on LD-203 reports in our sample. The sample of LD-203 reports we reviewed contained 80 reports with contributions and 80 reports without contributions. We estimate that overall for 2014, lobbyists failed to disclose one or more reportable contributions on 4 percent of reports.[10] Table 2 illustrates that from 2010 through 2014 most lobbyists disclosed FEC reportable contributions on their LD-203 reports as required. In 2014, nine LD-203 reports were amended in response to our review.

Table 2. Percentage of LD-203 Reports That Omitted One or More Political Contributions from 2010 through 2014

Year of review	2010	2011	2012	2013	2014
Number of reports with contributions that had one or more omissions	7	12	14	10[a]	8
Number of reports without contributions that had one or more omissions	1	2	4	0	1
Estimated percentage of all reports with one or more omissions	4%	9%	9%	4%	4%

Legend: n=80, except where noted with [a] where n=79.

Source: GAO analysis. | GAO-15-310

Note: These results contain contributions that are reportable to the Federal Election Commission. For this element in prior reports, we reported an estimated minimum percentage of reports based on a one-sided 95 percent confidence interval rather than the estimated proportion as shown here. Estimates in the table have a maximum margin of error of 9.5 percentage points.

Most Lobbying Firms Found It Easy to Comply with Disclosure Requirements and Understood Lobbying Terms

As part of our review, 93 different lobbying firms[11] were included in our 2014 sample of LD-2 disclosure reports.[12] Consistent with prior reviews, most lobbying firms reported that they found it "very easy" or "somewhat easy" to comply with reporting requirements. Of the 93 different lobbying firms in our sample, 16 reported that the disclosure requirements were "very easy," 54 reported them "somewhat easy," and 13 reported them "somewhat difficult" or "very difficult".[13] (See figure 10).

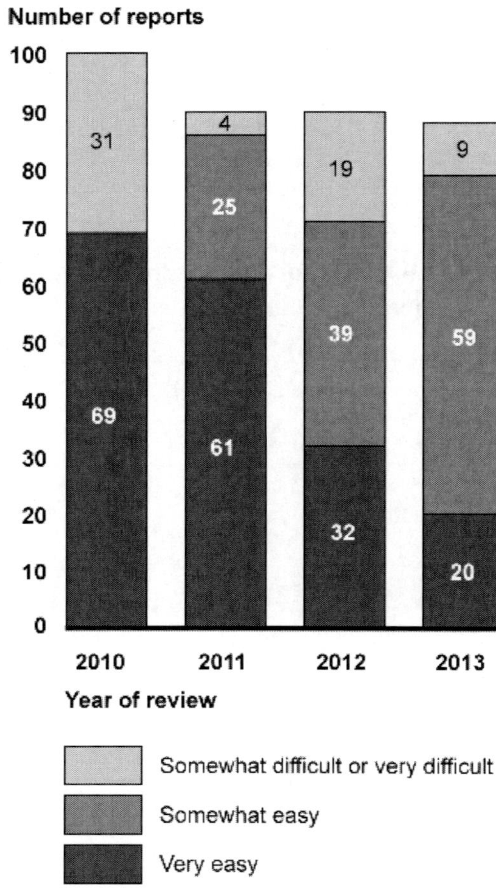

Source: GAO analysis. | GAO-15-310

Note: In 2011, our scale was as follows: "easy to meet," "somewhat easy to meet," or "difficult to meet." In 2010, we asked if it was "easy to comply" with disclosure requirements. For 2014, 10 of the 93 different lobbying firms did not respond to the question about ease of compliance with reporting requirements.

Figure 10. Ease of Complying with Lobbying Disclosure Requirements from 2010 through 2014.

Most lobbying firms we surveyed rated the definitions of terms used in LD-2 reporting as "very easy" or "somewhat easy" to understand with regard to meeting their reporting requirements. This is consistent with prior reviews. Figures 11 through 15 show what lobbyists reported as their ease of understanding the terms associated with LD-2 reporting requirements from 2010 through 2014.[14]

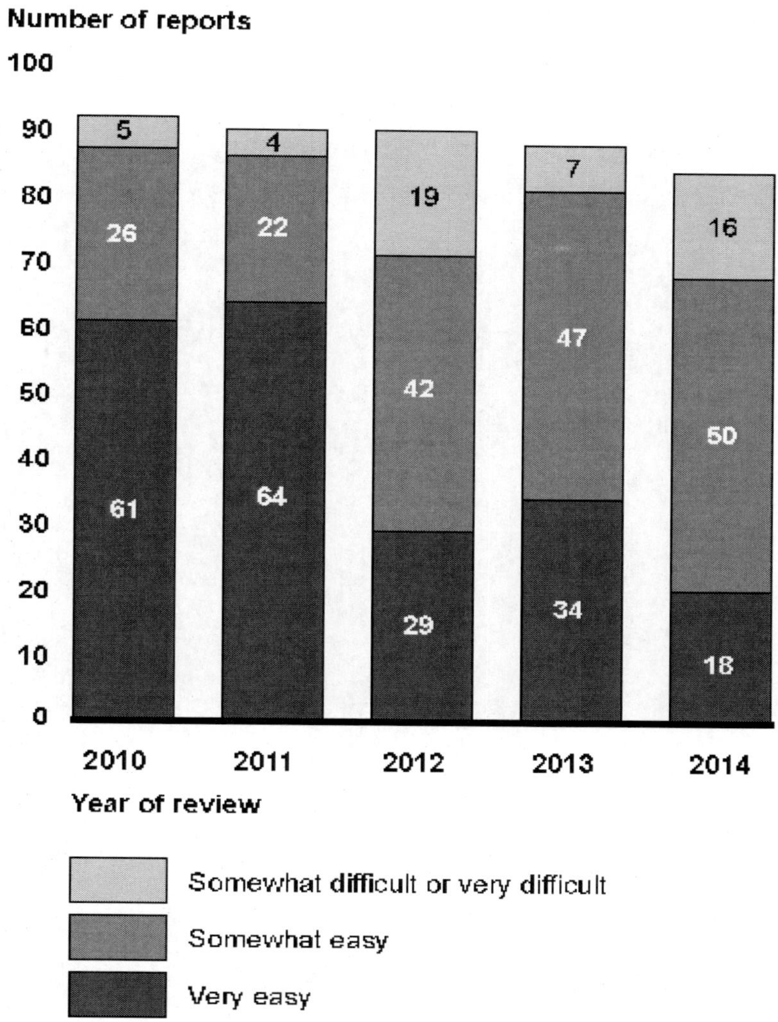

Source: GAO analysis. | GAO-15-310

Notes: In 2011 and 2010, we asked lobbyists to rate the terms associated with LD-2 reporting using the following scale: "clear and understandable," "somewhat clear and understandable," or "not clear and understandable."

Figure 11. Ease of Understanding Lobbying Definitions from 2010 through 2014.

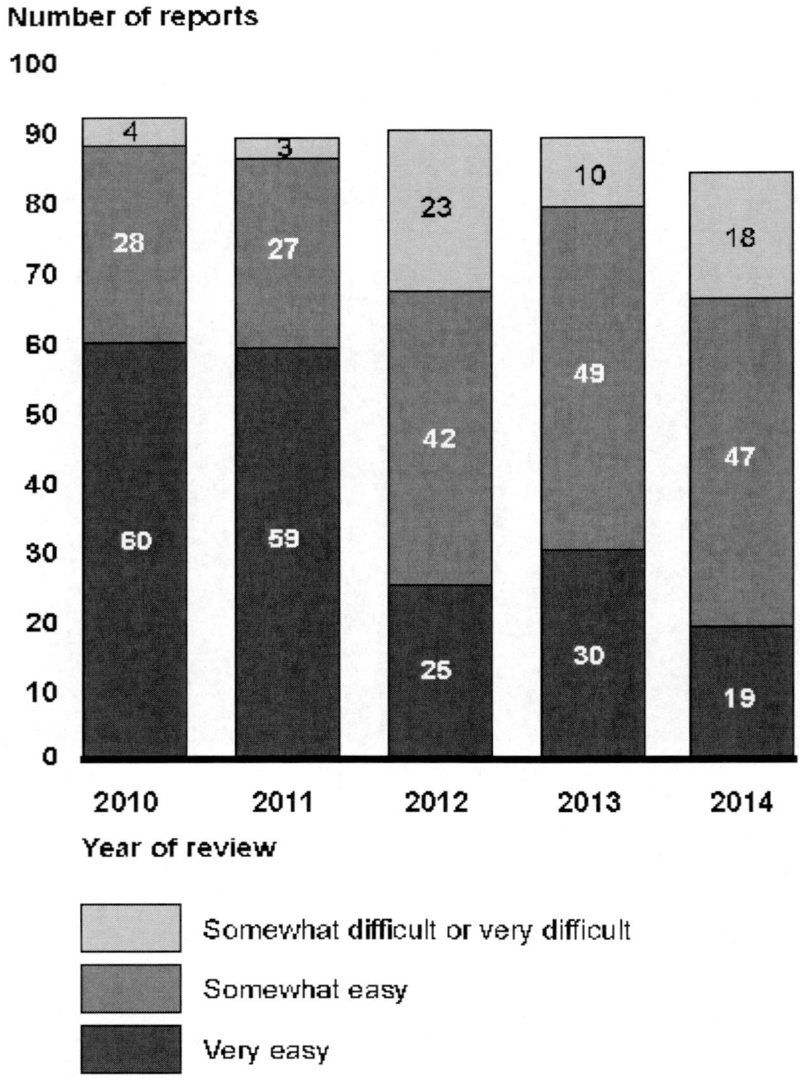

Source: GAO analysis. | GAO-15-310

Note: In 2011 and 2010, we asked lobbyists to rate the terms associated with LD-2 reporting using the following scale: "clear and understandable," "somewhat clear and understandable," or "not clear and understandable."

Figure 12. Ease of Understanding the Term "Lobbying Activities" from 2010 through 2014.

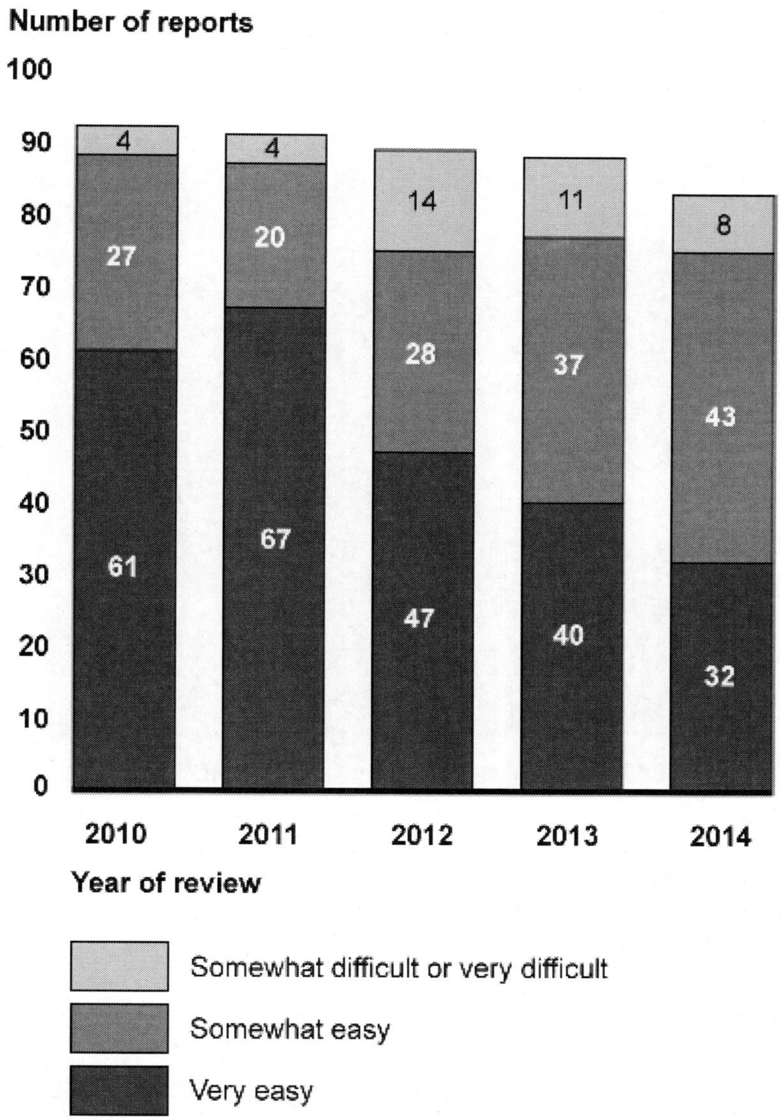

Source: GAO analysis. | GAO-15-310

Notes: In 2011 and 2010, we asked lobbyists to rate the terms associated with LD-2 reporting using the following scale: "clear and understandable," "somewhat clear" and "understandable," or "not clear and understandable." Issue codes are three letter codes for general lobbying topics such as education or agriculture.

Figure 13. Ease of Understanding Lobbying Issue Codes from 2010 through 2014.

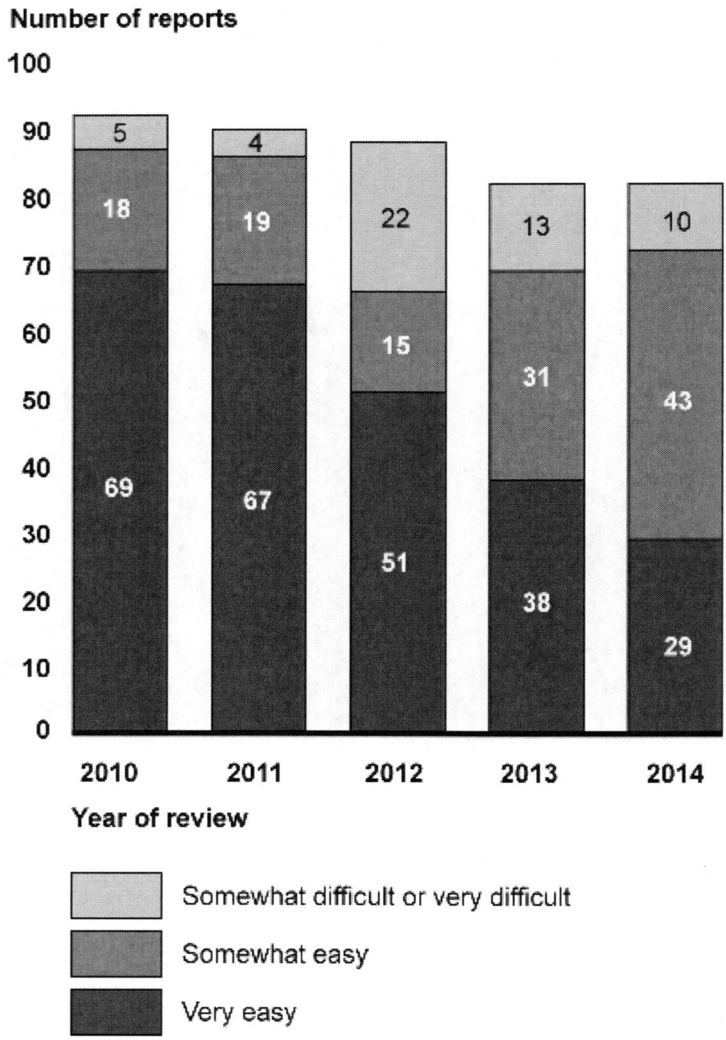

Source: GAO analysis. | GAO-15-310

Notes: In 2011 and 2010, we asked lobbyists to rate the terms associated with LD-2 reporting using the following scale: "clear and understandable" "somewhat clear and understandable," or "not clear and understandable." Covered positions are certain legislative and executive branch positions that the Honest Leadership and Open Government Act of 2007 requires a lobbyist to report as part of the disclosure process.

Figure 14. Ease of Understanding the Lobbying Term "Covered Positions" from 2010 through 2014.

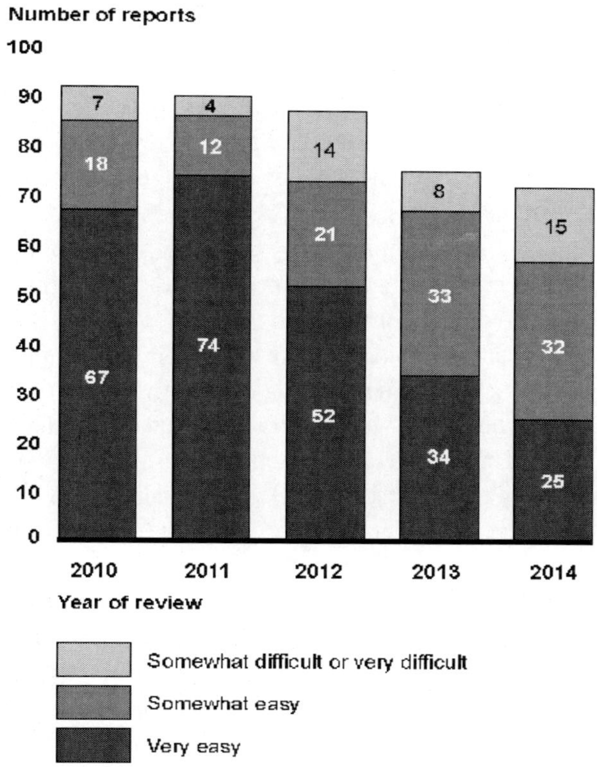

Source: GAO analysis. | GAO-15-310

Notes: In 2011 and 2010, we asked lobbyists to rate the terms associated with LD-2 reporting using the following scale: "clear and understandable," "somewhat clear and understandable," or "not clear and understandable." Terminating lobbyists means reporting that lobbyists previously listed as lobbying for a particular client are no longer lobbying for that client.

Figure 15. Ease of Understanding the Lobbying Term "Terminating Lobbyists" from 2010 through 2014.

U.S. Attorney's Office for the District of Columbia (USAO) Actions to Enforce the LDA

USAO's Resources and Authorities to Enforce LDA Compliance

USAO officials stated that they continue to have sufficient personnel resources and authority under the LDA to enforce reporting requirements, including imposing civil or criminal penalties for noncompliance. Noncompliance refers to a lobbyist's or lobbying firm's failure to comply with the LDA. According to USAO officials, they have one contract paralegal specialist assigned full time, as well as five civil attorneys and one criminal attorney assigned part time for LDA compliance work. In addition, USAO officials stated that the USAO participates in a program that provides Special Assistant United States Attorneys (SAUSA) to the USAO. Some of the SAUSAs assist with LDA compliance by working with the Assistant United States Attorneys and contract paralegal specialist to contact referred lobbyists or lobbying firms who do not comply with the LDA.

USAO officials stated that lobbyists resolve their noncompliance issues by filing LD-2s, LD-203s, LD-2 amendments, or by terminating their registration, depending on the issue. Resolving referrals can take anywhere from a few days to years, depending on the circumstances. During this time, USAO uses summary reports from its database to track the overall number of referrals that are pending or become compliant as a result of the lobbyist receiving an e-mail, phone call, or noncompliance letter. Referrals remain in the pending category until they are resolved. The category is divided into the following areas: "initial research for referral," "responded but not compliant," "no response/waiting for a response," "bad address," and "unable to locate." USAO focuses its enforcement efforts primarily on the responded but not compliant group. USAO attempts to review pending cases every 6 months, according to officials.

Officials told us that after four unsuccessful attempts have been made, USAO confers with both the Secretary of the Senate and the Clerk of the House to determine whether further action should be taken. In some cases where the lobbying firm is repeatedly referred for not filling disclosure reports but does not appear to be actively lobbying, USAO suspends enforcement actions. USAO monitors these firms, including checking the lobbying disclosure databases maintained by the Secretary of the Senate and the Clerk of the House. If the lobbyist begins to lobby again, USAO will resume enforcement actions.

Status of LD-2 Enforcement Efforts from 2009 through 2014 Reporting Periods

As of February 26, 2015, USAO has received 2,308 referrals from both the Secretary of the Senate and the Clerk of the House for failure to comply with LD-2 reporting requirements cumulatively for filing years 2009 through 2014. Table 3 shows the number and status of the referrals received and the number of enforcement actions taken by USAO in its effort to bring lobbying firms into compliance. Enforcement actions include the number of letters, e-mails, and calls made by USAO. About 52 percent (1,196 of 2,308) of the total referrals received are now compliant because lobbying firms either filed their reports or terminated their registrations. In addition, some of the referrals were found to be compliant when USAO received the referral. Therefore no action was taken. This may occur when lobbying firms respond to the contact letters from the Secretary of the Senate and Clerk of the House after USAO has received the referrals. About 48 percent (1,101 of 2,308) of referrals are pending further action because USAO was unable to locate the lobbying firm, did not receive a response from the firm, or plans to conduct additional research to determine if it can locate the lobbying firm. The remaining 11 referrals did not require action or were suspended because the lobbyist or client was no longer in business or the lobbyist was deceased.

Table 3. Status of Lobbying Disclosure Act Enforcement Actions for LD-2 Reporting from 2009 through 2014 (as of February 26, 2015)

Filing year	Referrals received	Referrals now compliant	Referrals pending further action	Referrals suspended or with deceased lobbyist	Enforcement actions on referrals received
2009	457	367	89	1	414
2010	446	371	65	10	349
2011	404	253	151	0	475
2012	451	159	292	0	333
2013	520	46	474	0	193
2014	30	0	30	0	0
Totals	2,308	1,196	1,101	11	1,764

Source: U.S. Attorney's Office for the District of Columbia. | GAO-15-310

Note: The referrals pending further action category is divided into the following areas: "initial research for referral," "responded but not compliant," "no response /waiting for a response," "bad address," and "unable to locate."

Status of LD-203 Enforcement Actions from 2009 through 2014 Reporting Periods

LD-203 referrals consist of two types: LD-203(R) referrals represent lobbying firms that have failed to file LD-203 reports for their lobbying firm; and LD-203 referrals represent the lobbyists at the lobbying firm who have failed to file their individual LD-203 reports as required. As of February 26, 2015, USAO had received 1,551 LD-203(R) referrals and 2,745 LD-203 referrals from the Secretary of the Senate and Clerk of the House for lobbying firms and lobbyists for noncompliance with reporting requirements cumulatively for calendar years 2009 through 2014.

LD-203 referrals may be more complicated than LD-2 referrals because both the lobbying firm and the individual lobbyists within the firm are each required to file a LD-203. However, according to USAO, lobbyists employed by a lobbying firm typically use the firm's contact information and not the lobbyists personal contact information. This makes it difficult to locate a lobbyist who may have left the firm. USAO reported that, while many firms have assisted it by providing contact information for lobbyists, they are not required to do so. According to officials, USAO has difficulty pursuing LD-203 referrals for lobbyists who have departed a firm without leaving forwarding contact information with the firm. While USAO utilizes web searches and online databases including LinkedIn, Lexis/Nexis, Glass Door, Facebook and the Sunlight Foundation websites to find these missing lobbyists, it is not always successful. When USAO is unable to locate lobbyists because it does not have forwarding contact information to find a lobbyist who has left a firm, USAO has no recourse to pursue enforcement action, according to officials.

Table 4 shows the status of LD-203 (R) referrals received and the number of enforcement actions taken by USAO in its effort to bring lobbying firms into compliance. About 46 percent (714 of 1,551) of the lobbying firms referred by the Secretary of the Senate and Clerk of the House for noncompliance from 2009 through 2014 reporting periods are now considered compliant because firms either have filed their reports or have terminated their registrations. About 54 percent (836 of 1,551) of the referrals are pending further action.

Table 4. Status of Lobbying Disclosure Act Enforcement Actions for LD-203(R) Lobbying Firms Only Reporting from 2009 through 2014 (as of February 26, 2015)

Filing year	Referrals received	Referrals now compliant	Referrals pending further action	Referrals suspended or with deceased lobbyist	Enforcement actions on referrals received
2009	151	106	45	0	79
2010	328	232	96	0	176
2011	403	241	162	0	294
2012	345	122	222	1	276
2013	324	13	311	0	3
2014	*	*	*	*	*
Totals	1,551	714	836	1	828

Legend: *No 2014 referrals have been received.

Source: U.S. Attorney's Office for the District of Columbia. | GAO-15-310

Note: The referrals pending further action category is divided into the following areas: "initial research for referral," "responded but not compliant," "no response /waiting for a response," "bad address," and "unable to locate."

Table 5 shows that as of February 26, 2015, USAO had received 2,745 LD-203 referrals from the Secretary of the Senate and Clerk of the House for lobbyists who failed to comply with LD-203 reporting requirements for calendar years 2009 through 2014. It also shows the status of the referrals received and the number of enforcement actions taken by USAO in its effort to bring lobbyists into compliance. In addition, table 5 shows that 44 percent (1,211 of 2,745) of the lobbyists had come into compliance by filing their reports or are no longer registered as a lobbyist. About 56 percent (1,525 of 2,745) of the referrals are pending further action because USAO was unable to locate the lobbyist, did not receive a response from the lobbyist, or plans to conduct additional research to determine if it can locate the lobbyist.

Table 6 shows that as of February 26, 2015, USAO had received LD-203 referrals from the Secretary of the Senate and Clerk of the House for 3,841 lobbyists who failed to comply with LD-203 reporting requirements for any filing year from 2009 through 2014. Table 6 shows the status of compliance for individual lobbyists listed on referrals to USAO. Table 6 shows that 48 percent (1,861 of 3,841 of the lobbyists had come into compliance by filing their reports or are no longer registered as a lobbyist. About 52 percent (1,980 of 3,841) of the referrals are pending action because USAO could not locate the lobbyists, did not receive a response from the lobbyists, or plans to conduct additional research to determine if it can locate the lobbyists.

Table 5. Status of Lobbying Disclosure Act Enforcement Actions for LD-203 Lobbyists Only Reporting from 2009 through 2014 (as of February 26, 2015)

Filing year	Number of referrals received	Referrals now compliant	Referrals pending further action	Referrals suspended or with deceased lobbyist	Enforcement actions on referrals received
2009	622	429	192	1	1,253
2010	1,228	664	556	8	636
2011	447	91	356	0	299
2012	273	27	246	0	49
2013	175	0	175	0	0
2014	*	*	*	*	*
Totals	2,745	1,211	1,525	9	2,237

Legend: *No 2014 referrals have been received.

Source: U.S. Attorney's Office for the District of Columbia. | GAO-15-310

Note: The referrals pending category is divided into the following areas: "initial research for referral," "responded but not compliant", "no response/waiting for a response," "bad address," and "unable to locate."

Table 6. Status of Lobbyist Compliance for LD-203 Lobbyist Only Referrals from 2009 through 2014 (as of February 26, 2015)

Filing year	Number of lobbyists on referrals received	Lobbyists now compliant on referrals received	Lobbyists still pending on referrals received
2009	980	685	295
2010	1,810	1,036	774
2011	542	108	434
2012	308	32	276
2013	201	0	201
2014	*	*	*
Totals	3,841	1,861	1,980

Legend: *No 2014 referrals have been received.

Source: U.S. Attorney's Office for the District of Columbia. | GAO-15-310

USAO officials said that many of the pending LD-203 referrals represent lobbyists who no longer lobby for the lobbying firms affiliated with the referrals, even though these lobbying firms may be listed on the lobbyist's LD-203 report.

Status of Enforcement Settlement Actions

According to USAO officials, lobbyists who repeatedly fail to file reports are labeled chronic offenders and referred to one of the assigned attorneys for follow-up. According to officials, USAO monitors and reviews chronic offenders to determine appropriate enforcement actions, which may lead to settlements or other successful civil actions. However, instead of pursuing a civil penalty, USAO may decide to pursue other actions such as closing out referrals if the lobbyist appears to be inactive. According to USAO, in these cases, there would be no benefit in pursuing enforcement actions.

USAO finalized a settlement in the amount of $30,000 for Alan Mauk & Alan Mauk Associates, Ltd to address failure to file for several years. According to officials USAO is close to finalizing a settlement with another firm for repeated failure to file.

AGENCY COMMENTS

We provided a draft of this report to the Attorney General for review and comment. The Department of Justice provided a technical comment, which we incorporated into the draft as appropriate.

J. Christopher Mihm
Managing Director, Strategic Issues

APPENDIX I: OBJECTIVES, SCOPE, AND METHODOLOGY

Our objectives were to determine the extent to which lobbyists are able to demonstrate compliance with the Lobbying Disclosure Act of 1995 as amended (LDA) by providing documentation to support information contained on registrations and reports filed under the LDA; to identify challenges and potential improvements to compliance, if any; and to describe the resources and authorities available to the U.S. Attorney's Office for the District of Columbia (USAO), its role in enforcing LDA compliance, and the efforts it has made to improve enforcement of the LDA.

We used information in the lobbying disclosure database maintained by the Clerk of the House of Representatives (Clerk of the House). To assess whether these disclosure data were sufficiently reliable for the purposes of this report, we reviewed relevant documentation and consulted with knowledgeable officials. Although registrations and reports are filed through a single web portal, each chamber subsequently receives copies of the data and follows different data-cleaning, processing, and editing procedures before storing the data in either individual files (in the House) or databases (in the Senate). Currently, there is no means of reconciling discrepancies between the two databases caused by the differences in data processing. For example, Senate staff told us during previous reviews they set aside a greater proportion of registration and report submissions than the House for manual review before entering the information into the database. As a result, the Senate database would be slightly less current than the House database on any given day pending review and clearance.

House staff told us during previous reviews that they rely heavily on automated processing. In addition, while they manually review reports that do not perfectly match information on file for a given lobbyist or client, staff members will approve and upload such reports as originally filed by each lobbyist, even if the reports contain errors or discrepancies (such as a variant on how a name is spelled). Nevertheless, we do not have reasons to believe that the content of the Senate and House systems would vary substantially. For this review, we determined that House disclosure data were sufficiently reliable for identifying a sample of quarterly disclosure (LD-2) reports and for assessing whether newly filed lobbyists also filed required reports. We used the House database for sampling LD-2 reports from the third and fourth quarters of 2013 and the first and second quarters of 2014, as well as for sampling year-end 2013 and mid-year 2014 political contributions (LD-203) reports. We also used the database for matching quarterly registrations with filed reports. We did not evaluate the Offices of the Secretary of the Senate or the Clerk of the House, both of which have key roles in the lobbying disclosure process. However, we did consult with officials from each office. They provided us with general background information at our request.

To assess the extent to which lobbyists could provide evidence of their compliance with reporting requirements, we examined a stratified random sample of 100 LD-2 reports from the third and fourth quarters of 2013 and the first and second quarters of 2014. We excluded reports with no lobbying activity or with income or expenses of less than $5,000 from our sampling frame.[1] We drew our sample from 46,599 activity reports filed for the third and fourth quarters of 2013 and the first and second quarters of 2014 available in the public House database, as of our final download date for each quarter.

Our sample of LD-2 reports was not designed to detect differences over time. However, we conducted tests of significance for changes from 2010 to 2014 for the generalizable elements of our review and found that results were generally consistent from year to year and there were few statistically significant changes after using a Bonferroni adjustment [2] to account for multiple comparisons. These changes are identified in the report. While the results provide some confidence that apparent fluctuations in our results across years are likely attributable to sampling error, the inability to detect significant differences may also be related to the nature of our sample, which was relatively small and was designed only for cross-sectional analysis.

Our sample is based on a stratified random selection and it is only one of a large number of samples that we may have drawn. Because each sample could have provided different estimates, we express our confidence in the precision of our particular sample's results as a 95 percent confidence interval. This interval would contain the actual population value for 95 percent of the samples that we could have drawn. The percentage estimates for LD-2 reports have a 95 percent confidence intervals of within plus or minus 12.1 percentage points or less of the estimate itself.

We contacted all the lobbyists and lobbying firms in our sample and, using a structured web-based survey, asked them to confirm key elements of the LD-2 and whether they could provide documentation for key elements in their reports, including

- the amount of income reported for lobbying activities;
- the amount of expenses reported on lobbying activities;
- the names of those lobbyists listed in the report;
- the houses of Congress and federal agencies that they lobbied and
- the issue codes listed to describe their lobbying activity.

After reviewing the survey results for completeness, we conducted interviews with the lobbyists and lobbying firms to review documentation they reported as having on their online survey for selected elements of their LD-2 report.

Prior to each interview, we conducted a search to determine whether lobbyists properly disclosed their covered position as required by the LDA. We reviewed the lobbyists' previous work histories by searching lobbying firms' websites, LinkedIn, Leadership Directories, Legistorm, and Google. Prior to 2008, lobbyists were only required to disclose covered official positions held within 2 years of registering as a lobbyist for the client. The Honest Leadership and Open Government Act of 2007 amended that time frame to require disclosure of positions held 20 years before the date the lobbyists first lobbied on behalf of the client. Lobbyists are required to disclose previously held covered official positions either on the client registration (LD-1) or on an LD-2 report. Consequently, those who held covered official positions may have disclosed the information on the LD-1 or a LD-2 report filed prior to the report we examined as part of our random sample. Therefore, where we found evidence that a lobbyist previously held a covered official position, and it was not disclosed on the LD-2 report under review, we conducted an additional review of the publicly available Secretary of the Senate or Clerk of the House database to determine whether the lobbyist properly disclosed the covered official position on a prior report or LD-1. Finally, if a lobbyist appeared to hold a covered position that was not disclosed, we asked for an explanation at the interview with the lobbying firm to ensure that our research was accurate.

In previous reports, we reported the lower bound of a 90 percent confidence interval to provide a minimum estimate of omitted covered positions and omitted contributions with a 95 percent confidence level. We did so to account for the possibility that our searches may have failed to identify all possible omitted covered positions and contributions. As we have developed our methodology over time, we are more confident in the comprehensiveness of our searches for these items. Accordingly, this report presents the estimated percentages for omitted contributions and omitted covered positions, rather than the minimum estimates. As a result, percentage estimates for these items will differ slightly from the minimum percentage estimates presented in prior reports.

In addition to examining the content of the LD-2 reports, we confirmed whether the most recent LD-203 reports had been filed for each firm and lobbyist listed on the LD-2 reports in our random sample. Although this review represents a random selection of lobbyists and firms, it is not a direct probability sample of firms filing LD-2 reports or lobbyists listed on LD-2 reports. As such, we did not estimate the likelihood that LD-203 reports were appropriately filed for the population of firms or lobbyists listed on LD-2 reports.

To determine if the LDA's requirement for lobbyists to file a report in the quarter of registration was met for the third and fourth quarters of 2013 and the first and second quarters of 2014, we used data filed with the Clerk of the House to match newly filed registrations with corresponding disclosure reports. Using an electronic matching algorithm that includes strict and loose text matching procedures, we identified matching disclosure reports for 2,659, or 90 percent, of the 2,950 newly filed registrations. We began by standardizing client and lobbyist names in both the report and registration files (including removing punctuation and standardizing words and abbreviations, such as "company" and "CO"). We then matched reports and registrations using the House identification number (which is linked to a unique lobbyist-client pair), as well as the names of the lobbyist and client.

For reports we could not match by identification number and standardized name, we also attempted to match reports and registrations by client and lobbyist name, allowing for variations in the names to accommodate minor misspellings or typos. For these cases, we used professional judgment to determine whether cases with typos were sufficiently similar to consider as matches. We could not readily identify matches in the report database for the remaining registrations using electronic means.

To assess the accuracy of the LD-203 reports, we analyzed stratified random samples of LD-203 reports from the 30,524 total LD-203 reports. The first sample contains 80 reports of the 9,787 reports with political contributions and the second contains 80 reports of the 20,737 reports listing no contributions. Each sample contains 40 reports from the yearend 2013 filing period and 40 reports from the midyear 2014 filing period. The samples from 2014 allow us to generalize estimates in this report to either the population of LD-203 reports with contributions or the reports without contributions to within a 95 percent confidence interval of plus or minus 9.5 percentage points or less. Although our sample of LD-203 reports was not designed to detect differences over time, we conducted tests of significance for changes from 2010 to 2014 and found no statistically significant differences after adjusting for multiple comparisons.[3]

While the results provide some confidence that apparent fluctuations in our results across years are likely attributable to sampling error, the inability to detect significant differences may also be related to the nature of our sample, which was relatively small and designed only for cross-sectional analysis. We analyzed the contents of the LD-203 reports and compared them to contribution data found in the publicly available Federal Elections Commission's (FEC) political contribution database. We consulted with staff at FEC responsible for administering the database. We determined that the data is sufficiently reliable for our purposes.

We compared the FEC-reportable contributions reporting on the LD-203 reports with information in the FEC database. The verification process required text and pattern matching procedures so we used professional judgment when assessing whether an individual listed is the same individual filing an LD-203. For contributions reported in the FEC database and not on the LD-203 report, we asked the lobbyists or organizations to explain why the contribution was not listed on the LD-203 report or to provide documentation of those contributions. As with covered positions on LD-2 disclosure reports, we cannot be certain that our review identified all cases of FEC-reportable contributions that were inappropriately omitted from a lobbyist's LD-203 report. We did not estimate the percentage of other non-FEC political contributions that were omitted because they tend to constitute a small minority of all listed contributions and cannot be verified against an external source.

To identify challenges to compliance, we used a structured web-based survey and obtained the views from 93 different lobbying firms included in our sample on any challenges to compliance. The number of different lobbying firms total 93 and is less than our sample of 100 reports because some lobbying firms had more than one LD-2 report included in our sample. We calculated our responses based on the number of different lobbying firms that we contacted rather than the number of interviews. Prior to our calculations, we removed the duplicate lobbying firms based on the most recent date of their responses. For those cases with the same response date, the decision rule was to keep the cases with the smallest assigned case identification number. To obtain their views, we asked them to rate their ease with complying with the LD-2 disclosure requirements using a scale, of "very easy," "somewhat easy," "somewhat difficult," or "very difficult." In addition, using the same scale we asked them to rate the ease of understanding the terms associated with LD-2 reporting requirements.

To describe the resources and authorities available to the U.S. Attorney's Office for the District of Columbia (USAO) and its efforts to improve its enforcement of the LDA, we interviewed officials from USAO. We obtained information on the capabilities of the system officials established to track and report compliance trends and referrals, and other practices established to focus resources on enforcement of the LDA. USAO provided us with updated reports from the tracking system on the number and status of referrals and chronically noncompliant lobbyists and lobbying firms.

The mandate does not require us to identify lobbyists who failed to register and report in accordance with the LDA requirements, or determine for those lobbyists who did register and report whether all lobbying activity or contributions were disclosed.

We conducted this performance audit from June 2014 to March 2015 in accordance with generally accepted government auditing standards. Those standards require that we plan and perform the audit to obtain sufficient, appropriate evidence to provide a reasonable basis for our findings and conclusions based on our audit objectives. We believe that the evidence obtained provides a reasonable basis for our findings and conclusions based on our audit objectives.

APPENDIX II: LIST OF LOBBYISTS AND CLIENTS FOR SAMPLED LOBBYING DISCLOSURE REPORTS

The random sample of lobbying disclosure reports we selected was based on unique combinations of lobbyist and client names (see table 7).

Table 7. Names of Lobbyists and Clients Selected in Random Sample of Lobbying Disclosure Reports Filed in the Third and Fourth Quarters of 2013 and First and Second Quarters of 2014

Lobbyist name	Client
38 North Solutions, LLC	MIOX Corporation
ADS Ventures, Inc.	Putnam Investments
Aduston Consulting, LLC	National Religious Broadcasters Music License Committee
Airbus America, Inc. (formerly Airbus North America Holdings, Inc.)	Airbus America, Inc. (formerly Airbus North America Holdings, Inc.)
Akerman LLP (formally known as Akerman Senterfitt)	Vidler Water Company
Akin Gump Strauss Hauer & Feld	Black Business Investment Fund of Central Florida, Inc.
Akin Gump Strauss Hauer & Feld	Corrections Corporation of America
Alcalde & Fay	City of Hallandale Beach

Table 7. (Continued)

Lobbyist name	Client
Alpine Group, Inc.	High Tech Spectrum Coalition
American Association of Nurse Practitioners	American Association of Nurse Practitioners
Americans for Responsible Solutions	Americans for Responsible Solutions
Association of the United States Army, Inc.	Association of the United States Army, Inc.
Ball Janik LLP	Port of Hood River, Oregon
Barnes & Thornburg LLP	Health & Hospital Corporation of Marion County
Capitol Counsel LLC	Regions Financial Corp.
Capitol Hill Consulting Group	Secure ID Coalition
Capitol Tax Partners, LLP	National Council of Farmer Cooperatives
Capitol Tax Partners, LLP	State Street Bank & Trust Company
Cassidy & Associates, Inc. (formerly known as Cassidy & Associates)	Iowa State University
Chambers, Conlon & Hartwell, LLC	Rajant Corporation
CJ Lake, LLC	Fresno Community Hospital and Medical Center (formerly CommunityMed. Centers)
Clark Geduldig Cranford & Nielsen	Organization for International Investment
Cornerstone Government Affairs, LLC	The Cherokee Nation
Crossroads Strategies, LLC	Genentech, Inc.
Daley Policy Group, LLC	Northern Illinois University
David Turch & Associates	City of Torrance, CA
Davidoff Hutcher & Citron LLP	Center for Educational Innovation-Public Education Association (CEI-PEA)
Dentons US LLP	UCare
Dickstein & Shapiro, LLP	National Association of the Remodeling Industry
DiNino Associates, LLC	MAXIMUS

Lobbyist name	Client
DLA Piper LLP (US)	Coalition on Health Care
Emory University	Emory University
Foley & Lardner LLP	Aurora Healthcare
Forbes-Tate	American Sportfishing Association
Gephardt Group Government Affairs	UnitedHealth Group, Inc.
Guidry Associates LLC	St. John the Baptist Parish
Heather McNatt Hennessey LLC	GPS Innovation Alliance
Hobbs, Straus, Dean & Walker, LLP	Prairie Band of Potawatomi Nation
Hogan Lovells US LLP	Primus Holdings Limited
Hurt, Norton & Associates, Inc.	Daniel Defense
Innovative Federal Strategies, LLC	Florida Institute For Human and Machine Cognition
International Business-Government Counselors, Inc. [aka IBC]	MTB Coalition [information coalition]
International Myeloma Foundation	International Myeloma Foundation
Jones Walker LLP	FM Services CO
Jones Walker LLP	Intermarine, LLC
K&L Gates LLP	Consortium of State Maritime Academies
K&L Gates LLP	RenaissanceRe Holdings Ltd.
Kadesh & Associates, LLC	Tejon Ranch Company
Katharine Armstrong, Inc.	Texas Oil and Gas Association (TXOGA)
Kearney, Donovan & McGee	New England Center for Children
King & Spalding LLP	Embraer Empresa Brasileira de Aeronautica S.A.
Law Offices of Mark S. Joffe	Medicare Cost Contractors Alliance
Madison Associates, LLC	Council Of Infrastructure Financing Authorities
Manatt, Phelps, and Phillips	Big Heart Pet Food (f.k.a. Del Monte)
Masco Corporation	Masco Corporation
McBee Strategic Consulting, LLC.	Schrader International, Inc.
Millennium: The Takeda Oncology Company	Millennium: The Takeda Oncology Company
ML Strategies, LLC	American Well Corporation

Table 7. (Continued)

Lobbyist name	**Client**
ML Strategies, LLC	Iberdrola Renewables
Mr. Glenn Roger Delaney	Southern Shrimp Alliance
Mr. John T O'Rourke	H&R Block Inc.
Mr. Richard Goodstein	Air Products and Chemicals, Inc.
Mr. Richard Miller	Association of Health Sciences Colleges And Universities
National Coalition For History	National Coalition For History
National Cooperative Services Corporation	National Cooperative Services Corporation
National Group LLP	Makai Licensing and Finance, LLC
National Ocean Industries Association	National Ocean Industries Association
Navigators Global LLC (Formerly DC Navigators, LLC)	Alliant Techsystems Inc.
Ogilvy Government Relations	Network Branded Prepaid Card Association
Oldaker Group, LLC	National Association of Marine Laboratories
Orion Associates	Renewable Bag Council
PBF Holding Company LLC	PBF Holding Company LLC
Peck Madigan Jones	AbbVie Inc.
Peck Madigan Jones	The Hertz Corporation
Phillips 66	Phillips 66
Podesta Group, Inc.	Optical Society of America
Primerica Life Insurance Company	Primerica Life Insurance Company
RM2 Consultants, Inc.	L-3 Chesapeake Sciences Corporation
Robertson, Monagle & Eastaugh	City of Unalaska
Shockey Scofield Solutions, LLC	American Silencer Association
Simon and Company	Louisville, Kentucky
Small Business & Entrepreneurship Council (SBE Council)	Small Business & Entrepreneurship Council (SBE Council)
Sorini, Samet, & Associates, LLC	Payless ShoeSource
Spectra Energy	Spectra Energy
Squire Patton Boggs (formerly Patton Boggs)	Assured Guaranty

Lobbyist name	Client
Steptoe & Johnson LLP	1800 CONTACTS
Steptoe & Johnson LLP	EtaGen
Strategic Marketing Innovations, Inc.	Columbia Power Technologies
The D Major Group	University Hospitals Health System Inc.
The New England Council	The New England Council
The Russell Group, Inc.	Land O'Lakes, Inc.
Thompson Hine LLP	Texas Biomedical Research Institute
Tompkins Strategies, LLC	Aircraft Owners & Pilots Association (AOPA)
Urban Swirski & Associates, LLC	Emerson Electric Co.
VH Strategies, LLC	Arch Coal
Van Ness Feldman, LLP	Public Utility District No 1 Of Snohomish County
Van Scoyoc Associates	American Association of Homeopathic Pharmacists
Vitello Consulting	Barona Band of Mission Indians
Wexler & Walker Public Policy Associates	ABB (formerly Asea Brown BoveriI, Inc.)
Williams and Jensen, PLLC	Hickey Freeman Tailored Clothing, Inc

Source: Lobbying disclosure database of the Clerk of the House of Representatives for the third and fourth quarters of calendar year 2013 and the first and second quarters of calendar year 2013. | GAO-15-310

Appendix III: List of Sampled Lobbying Contribution Reports with and without Contributions Listed

See table 8 for a list of the lobbyists and lobbying firms from our random sample of lobbying contributions reports with contributions. See table 9 for a list of the lobbyists and lobbying firms from our random sample of lobbying contribution reports without contributions.

Table 8. Lobbyists and Lobbying Firms in Sample of Lobbying Contribution Reports with Contributions Listed, Filed Year-end 2013 and Mid-year 2014

Lobbyist or lobbying firm	Reporting period
Adrien Rivard III	Year-end 2013
Albemarle Corporation	Year-end 2013
Alcoa, Inc.	Year-end 2013
Alejandro Urrea	Mid-year 2014
Allen Greenwood Jr.	Mid-year 2014
American Health Care Association	Mid-year 2014
Amy Muhlberg	Year-end 2013
Applied Materials, Inc	Mid-year 2014
Arienne Brint	Year-end 2013
Athan Manuel	Year-end 2013
Baker & Botts, LLP	Mid-year 2014
Ball Janik LLP	Year-end 2013
Barbara Mattox	Year-end 2013
Bethany Bassett	Mid-year 2014
Brenda Luckritz	Year-end 2013
Brian Pomper	Mid-year 2014
Bunge North America, Inc	Mid-year 2014
Chester Lott Sr.	Year-end 2013
Daniel Cunningham	Year-end 2013
David Franasiak	Mid-year 2014
Davis Wright Tremaine LLP	Year-end 2013
Direct Marketing Association, Inc.	Mid-year 2014
Drew Cantor	Year-end 2013
Edward Kussy	Year-end 2013
Elbit Systems Of America, LLC	Mid-year 2014
Eric Kessler	Year-end 2013
FMC Corporation	Mid-year 2014
George Salem	Year-end 2013
Great Plains Energy (Formerly Kansas City Power & Light)	Mid-year 2014
Hector Alcalde	Mid-year 2014
Huntington Ingalls Industries Incorporated	Year-end 2013
International Brotherhood Of Teamsters	Mid-year 2014
Intl. Assn. Of Amusement Pks. & Attrs.	Year-end 2013

Lobbyist or lobbying firm	Reporting period
James Dennis	Mid-year 2014
James Dykstra	Year-end 2013
Jay Brown	Year-end 2013
Jay Ghazal	Year-end 2013
Jeff Mackinnon	Year-end 2013
Jeffrey Peck	Mid-year 2014
Jennifer Luray	Mid-year 2014
Jessica Mandel	Mid-year 2014
John Lagomarcino	Year-end 2013
Jon Beamer	Mid-year 2014
Joseph Vaughan	Mid-year 2014
Kathleen Black	Mid-year 2014
Kenneth Levine	Year-end 2013
Larry Rosenthal	Year-end 2013
Lonnie Johnson	Year-end 2013
Maria Cino	Mid-year 2014
Mary Sprayregen	Year-end 2013
Merck & Co, Inc.	Year-end 2013
Michael Torra	Mid-year 2014
Michele Lieber	Mid-year 2014
Mitch Glazier	Year-end 2013
Mona Sheth	Mid-year 2014
Mr. Hector Alcalde	Year-end 2013
Nancy Dorn	Year-end 2013
National Air Carrier Association	Year-end 2013
National Funeral Directors Assn	Mid-year 2014
National Right To Life Committee	Mid-year 2014
New York Farm Bureau, Inc.	Mid-year 2014
Nicole Venable	Mid-year 2014
Northeast Utilities Service Company	Year-end 2013
Paul Donovan	Year-end 2013
Paul Moorehead	Mid-year 2014
Premier, Inc.	Year-end 2013
Rai Services Company	Mid-year 2014
Randel Johnson	Year-end 2013
Ryan Haaker	Mid-year 2014
Salesforce.Com	Year-end 2013
Sam Geduldig	Mid-year 2014

Table 8. (Continued)

Lobbyist or lobbying firm	Reporting period
Samuel Horton	Mid-year 2014
Scott Faber	Mid-year 2014
Stanley Rapp	Year-end 2013
The American Institute Of Architects	Mid-year 2014
Thomas Turner	Year-end 2013
Timothy Costa	Mid-year 2014
UPS	Year-end 2013
Zimmer, Inc.	Mid-year 2014
Zurich	Mid-year 2014

Source: Lobbying contributions database of the Clerk of the House of Representatives, year-end reports for calendar year 2013 and mid-year reports for calendar year 2014. | GAO-15-310

Table 9. Lobbyists and Lobbying Firms in Random Sample of Lobbying Contribution Reports without Contributions Listed, Filed Year-end 2013 and Mid-year 2014

Lobbyist or lobbying firm	Filing period
Alanna Suda	Mid-year 2014
Amanda Uherek	Year-end 2013
American Bird Conservancy	Mid-year 2014
Association For Corporate Growth, Inc.	Mid-year 2014
Bar Education	Year-end 2013
Bennet & Bennet, PLLC	Mid-year 2014
Bob Barr	Year-end 2013
Bromelkamp Government Relations, LLC	Year-end 2013
Capcity Advocates, LLC	Mid-year 2014
Christopher Hessler	Mid-year 2014
Christopher Topoleski	Year-end 2013
Christpher Gregory	Mid-year 2014
Council For Citizens Against Government Waste	Year-end 2013
David Lindsay	Mid-year 2014
David Pietsch	Mid-year 2014
Debra Barrett	Mid-year 2014
Devry Boughner	Year-end 2013
Douglas Read	Year-end 2013

Lobbyist or lobbying firm	Filing period
Duane Musser	Year-end 2013
Electricity Consumers Resource Council (ELCON)	Year-end 2013
Elizabeth Brooks	Year-end 2013
Ellen Riker	Mid-year 2014
Environmental Industry Associations	Year-end 2013
Erik Huey	Mid-year 2014
Frazer Burkart	Year-end 2013
Friends Of The Global Fight Against Aids, Tuberculosis And Malaria	Mid-year 2014
Herschel Hawley	Mid-year 2014
James Hadel	Year-end 2013
Janet Lambert	Year-end 2013
Jeff Hennie	Mid-year 2014
Jerry Weiss	Year-end 2013
Joel Widder	Year-end 2013
Jonathan Weisgall	Year-end 2013
Jordan Moon	Year-end 2013
Julia Drost	Mid-year 2014
Karen Studwell	Year-end 2013
Katherine Berland	Mid-year 2014
Kathryn Hollister	Year-end 2013
Kountoupes Denham (Formerly Reporting As Kountoupes Consulting, LLC)	Mid-year 2014
Kristen Freitas	Mid-year 2014
Ladeene Freimuth	Mid-year 2014
Lisa Heyn	Year-end 2013
Lynden Melmed	Year-end 2013
Manufactured Housing Association For Regulatory Reform	Year-end 2013
Mark O'Connell	Mid-year 2014
Matt Willette	Mid-year 2014
Matthew Pickering	Mid-year 2014
Michael Levas	Mid-year 2014
Michael Matlack	Mid-year 2014
Michelle Neblett	Year-end 2013
Motorola Mobility, LLC	Year-end 2013
MPC Consulting	Year-end 2013
Mr. Robert Seraphin	Year-end 2013

Table 9. (Continued)

Lobbyist or lobbying firm	Filing period
Mr. Timothy James	Year-end 2013
Nassau Suffolk Hospital Council	Mid-year 2014
Nicholas Gentile	Mid-year 2014
Nicole Hendrickson	Year-end 2013
Omar Nashashibi	Year-end 2013
Patric Link	Mid-year 2014
Paul Snyder	Year-end 2013
Ralph Palmieri	Mid-year 2014
R-Calf United Stockgrowers Of America	Mid-year 2014
Rebecca O'Connor	Year-end 2013
Rene Campos	Year-end 2013
Robert Barnett	Year-end 2013
Robert Filippone	Year-end 2013
Roxanne Brown	Year-end 2013
Ruthanne Goodman	Mid-year 2014
Ryan Ullman	Mid-year 2014
Shearman & Sterling, LLP	Mid-year 2014
Shimere Williams	Mid-year 2014
Stephanie Henning	Mid-year 2014
Stephen Wood	Mid-year 2014
Terrence Heubert	Year-end 2013
The Mondello Group LLC	Mid-year 2014
Theodore Kronmiller	Mid-year 2014
Thomas Downs	Mid-year 2014
Todd Howe	Mid-year 2014
Will Marsh	Year-end 2013
William Rys	Year-end 2013

Source: Lobbying contributions database of the Clerk of the House of Representatives, year-end reports for calendar year 2013 and mid-year reports for calendar year 2014. | GAO-15-310

End Notes

[1] Pub. L. No. 110-81, 121 Stat. 735 (Sept. 14, 2007) (2 U.S.C. §§ 1601-1614).

[2] 2 U.S.C. § 1614.

[3] Our sample is only one of a large number of samples that we might have drawn. Because each sample could have provided different estimates, we express our confidence in the precision of our estimate as a 95 percent confidence interval. This interval would contain the actual population value for 95 percent of the samples we could have drawn. Unless otherwise stated, all percentage estimates have a maximum 95 percent confidence interval of within 12.1 percentage points or less of the estimate.

[4] Although we contacted each lobbying firm, lobbying sole proprietorship, and organization with in-house lobbyists in our sample, we did not always meet with the lobbyists identified as the point of contact or with the actual lobbyists. We met with individuals representing the lobbyists in our sample. For the purposes of this review, we use the term lobbyists to refer to lobbyists, lobbying firms, organizations with in-house lobbyists, and individuals representing the lobbyists who were present during the review.

[5] 2 U.S.C. § 1602(10). The LDA defines a covered executive branch official as the President, Vice President, an officer or employee, or any other individual functioning in the capacity of such an officer or employee of the Executive Office of the President; an officer or employee serving in levels I through V of the Executive Schedule; members of the uniformed services whose pay grade is at or above O-7; and any officer or employee serving in a position of a confidential, policy-determining, policy-making or policy-advocating character who is excepted from competitive service as determined by the Office of Personnel Management (commonly called Schedule C employees). The LDA defines a covered legislative branch official as a member of Congress, an elected officer of either house of Congress, or any employee or any other individual functioning in the capacity of an employee of a member, a committee of either house of Congress, the leadership staff of either house of Congress, a joint committee of Congress, or a working group or caucus organized to provide legislative services or other assistance to members. 2 U.S.C. § 1602(3), (4). Lobbying activities include not only direct lobbying contacts but also efforts in support of such contacts, such as preparation and planning activities, research, and other background work that is intended for use in contacts. 2 U.S.C. § 1602(7).

[6] 2 U.S.C. § 1602(9).

[7] Organizations employing in-house lobbyists file only one registration. An organization is exempt from filing if total expenses in connection with lobbying activities are not expected to exceed $12,500. Amounts are adjusted for inflation and published in LDA guidance.

[8] Under the LDA Guidance, both the lobbying firm reporting income and the organizations reporting expenses are to provide a good faith estimate of the actual dollar amount rounded to the nearest $10,000. Our estimate of the number of reports with rounding errors includes reports that disclosed the exact amount of income from or expenditures on lobbying activities, but failed to round to the nearest $10,000 as required.

[9] The sample size of LD-2 reports that reported contact with federal agencies is smaller than the 100 LD-2 reports that were included in our sample and used to generate percentage sums for other selected reporting elements. The size is also too small to generate estimated percentages or to make comparisons across the reviews.

[10] We did not estimate the percentage of other nonFEC political contributions that were omitted because they tend to constitute a small minority of all listed contributions and cannot be verified against an external data source.

[11] The use of the term "lobbying firms" in this context includes organizations with in-house lobbyists.

[12] The number of different lobbying firms total 93 and is less than our sample of 100 reports because some lobbying firms had more than one LD-2 report included in our sample. We

calculated our responses based on the number of different lobbying firms that we contacted rather than the number of interviews. Prior to our calculations, we removed the duplicate lobbying firms based on the most recent date of their responses. For those cases with the same response date, we kept the cases with the smallest assigned case identification number.

[13] Of the 93 different lobbying firms, 10 did not respond to the question about ease of compliance with reporting requirements. Although the percentage estimates from our sample of LD-2 reports are generalizable to all LD-2 reports, results from the analysis of lobbying firm opinions are not generalizable. Our sample was designed to develop population estimates of the accuracy of information on LD-2 reports. It was not designed to estimate lobbyist opinions.

[14] Some lobbying firms may not have responded to all of the questions about their ease of understanding the terms associated with LD-2 reporting requirements. Therefore the number of responses may not be consistent with the number of different lobbying firms in figures 11 through 15.

End Notes for Appendix I

[1] LD-2 activity reports with "no lobbying issue activity" and reports with less than $5,000 in reported income or expenses are filtered out because they do not contain verifiable information on income, expenses, or activity.

[2] A Bonferroni adjustment is a statistical adjustment designed to reduce the chance of making a type 1 inferential error, that is, concluding that a difference exists when it is instead an artifact of sampling error. The adjustment raises the threshold for concluding that any single difference is "statistically significant" so that overall the chance of making at least one type-1 error when making multiple comparisons does not exceed a specified level.

[3] We used a Bonferroni adjustment to adjust for three comparisons to account for the three pairwise tests for each item examined.

INDEX

D

E

F

R

S

T

U

V

W